Geoffrey Parker, M.A.
Extramural Tutor, University of Birmingham
Formerly Lecturer in Geography
Tottenham Technical College

The Geography of
Economics

A WORLD SURVEY

Second Edition

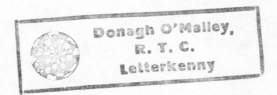

LONGMAN

LONGMAN GROUP LIMITED
London
Associated companies, branches and
representatives throughout the world

© *Geoffrey Parker 1965*
This edition © *Longman Group Limited 1972*

First published 1965
Second impression 1967
Third impression 1969
Second edition 1972

A/330.9

ISBN 0 582 41030 4 *Cased*
ISBN 0 582 41031 2 *Paper*

Set in 10 pt Plantin by Eta Services, Beccles
and printed in Great Britain by Hazell, Watson & Viney Ltd., Aylesbury.

Contents

Maps and Diagrams

Tables

Plates

Acknowledgements

We are grateful to the following for permission to reproduce copyright material:

The Clarendon Press for material from *Climates of the Continents* by W. G. Kendrew, and Hutchinson & Co. (Publishers) Ltd for material from *The Geography of Iron and Steel* by Norman J. G. Pounds.

Preface

THIS book is designed to meet the needs of students of Economic Geography, and especially those who are engaged in economics and business courses. It therefore contains a number of individual features not previously encountered in books of this type. In its preparation three principles have all along been borne in mind. These are that it should be *relevant*; that it should be *selective*; and that it should be *practical*.

By the first principle is meant not only relevance to the needs of examination candidates, which must naturally be a basic consideration, but also to the other courses they are studying and to the world scene as a whole. To help achieve this, Chapter 1, The World Background, contains an outline of economic, political and social matters which are of considerable importance today. Such questions as these are now as relevant as are physical factors to an understanding of the world's economic geography. The physical background is treated only briefly at the beginning, and the classification of the world's climates has been put in Appendix 1. It is intended that this should be used freely for reference throughout the course.

The book is selective in that it does not attempt to deal with the whole world in an equal degree of detail. The provision simply of a generalised 'bird's eye view' would lend itself to over-simplification, and be alien to the aim of encouraging the student to find out information for himself. Besides, with the excellent atlases and reference books available today, it is neither necessary nor desirable that the textbook should attempt to contain everything within its covers. This book is therefore designed to stimulate the student's curiosity in what this interesting subject has to offer, and to complement, rather than attempt to dispense with, the work of the lecturer or teacher. It is believed that what really counts is not cramming facts but developing an attitude of mind, and to do this an attempt is made to demonstrate geographical principles as they are seen at work in all parts of the world. Examples are chosen to illustrate particular phenomena, and end-of-chapter questions often demand the application to certain areas of the principles learned in studying others. The very full index and reference section at the end is intended to help the student co-ordinate the various aspects of his work. The whole world has been treated in as balanced a manner as possible, but the features of Great Britain's economic geography have purposely been given in considerable detail.

Geography is essentially a visual and practical subject. The student is therefore given a considerable amount of practical work, with a view to the interpretation of the material contained in maps and diagrams. An outline of the techniques of map and diagram drawing is given in Appendix 2. I consider it very inadequate merely to let the student see visual techniques such as graphs and proportional diagrams and leave it at that. He must be encouraged to produce them for himself, and by so doing learn to use and understand them better.

This book will be found especially suitable for use with professional courses such as the Ordinary National Diploma and Certificate in Business Studies and the Certificate of the Institute of Bankers. It is also suitable for use with G.C.E. Advanced Level Courses in Economic Geography. The integration of practical exercises with the text should prove a special attraction for the G.C.E. work. I have been guided constantly by the views expressed by the Further Education Section of the Geographical Association. This body has long studied the question of teaching economic geography to students, and the enlightened ideas which have been the result of this have helped me immensely in assessing the type of book which is likely to be best adapted to present requirements.

Finally I must express my indebtedness to a large number of industrial and other organisations which have most kindly made available to me a wealth of statistical and other information. I wish particularly to thank the following: The Petroleum Information Bureau; Shipbuilding Conference; Society of Motor Manufacturers and Traders; Cotton Board; British Man-Made Fibres Federation; Cement and Concrete Association; Commonwealth Economic Commission; High Commission of Australia. The information for Table 12 is by kind permission of the Geographical Association. Considerable use has been made of the statistics published by the various agencies of the United Nations, and all the figures for world production and trade are the most recent available.

I am also obliged to the many friends and colleagues who have been so helpful, and I owe a special debt of gratitude to my wife who has, at all stages, taken an active part in the preparation of the book and has compiled the index.

GEOFFREY PARKER

Preface to the Second Edition

Since this book was first published many changes have taken place in the world's economic geography, and it is the intention of this new edition to reflect these. The most recent available information has been included and as a consequence it has been necessary to change and re-write many sections.

A major change is in the use of metric (SI) units of measurement. These are now used for temperature, rainfall, distance and area, and the Imperial equivalents are given in brackets. Only in the list of sample climatic stations given in Appendix 1 have Fahrenheit and inches been retained as the principal units, but this is followed by a table of equivalents (Appendix 2) which makes it easy to convert these into centigrade and millimetres. The process of changing to the metric system will undoubtedly take a long time, and it is therefore not considered advisable to dispense completely with familiar measurements as yet. Students must be taught to think metric, and constant references between the two systems are an essential part of training to do this.

GEOFFREY PARKER

Lichfield, 1971

Chapter 1
The World Background

WE are living in an age when great changes are affecting all aspects of human activity. The forces which have been steadily gathering during the first half of the present century have burst forth since the Second World War, and are in process of altering the whole of the human way of life. In science man has achieved things which were in the realms of fiction only two decades ago. The advances in industry have been of a rapidity unprecedented in the whole of human history. The earth has shrunk as it has been spanned by jet air routes which can take people thousands of miles in a matter of hours, and motor roads which can make even the remotest areas accessible. Politically the changes have been no less dramatic, with the great world empires centred on Europe disintegrating and being replaced by a crop of sovereign states. Now, for the first time in four centuries, Europe has ceased to be the major centre of human progress. Meanwhile, new powers have emerged which are of continental dimensions and possess immense resources. Socially the principle of human equality has been accepted over most of the world, and exaggerated differences of wealth and social status have been reduced.

It is against this background of rapid changes that we have to study the economic geography of the world, because the production and distribution of raw materials and manufactures must be influenced by the conditions in which it is taking place. It, in turn, can help us to understand the workings of the world economic system, and to realise more fully the interdependence of all parts of the world.

THE OLD EMPIRES

The great empires centring on Western Europe have provided the framework within which the system of worldwide trade has been built.

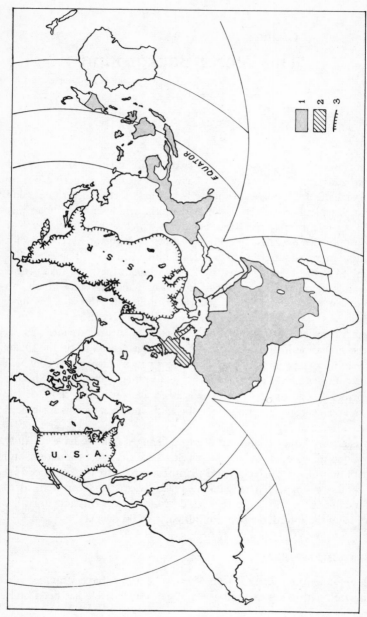

Fig. 1. The Political Background. 1. Former dependent territories which have become independent countries since 1945. 2. The countries (in Europe only) from which they have gained independence. 3. USA and USSR the 'Super Powers'

They resulted from the spread of European influence between the sixteenth and the nineteenth centuries, during which the European nations found it necessary to bring those parts of the globe with which they had trade relations more and more under their direct control. By the end of the nineteenth century only two extensive areas, the Far East and the Middle East, had not been colonised by Europeans. This was the height of the period of 'imperialism', when the possession of an empire ceased to be regarded as a burden and became a national status symbol and a source of pride. Latecomers such as Germany and Italy vied with older colonial powers such as Great Britain, France, Belgium and the Netherlands in snatching what territories were still unclaimed. These unwieldy empires, paramount among which was the British, were kept together by the use of the seas for commerce and naval power. The British prided themselves on an empire on which 'the sun never set', and there was much talk of the civilising mission of the European peoples. By 1914 about 55 per cent of the world's land area came within these empires.

The empires owed much of their strength to the powerlessness of the native populations at the time, and as these became stronger and more politically aware, so they began to demand independence. This was no new thing; indeed, the United States had become independent of England in the late eighteenth century, and after this she invariably recognised that her overseas territories would ultimately achieve self-government. The old British dominions were the first to attain to independence, and it was not until after the Second World War that the other European nations began to divest themselves of their possessions (Fig. 1). The final stage in the process began with the granting of independence to the Indian subcontinent in 1947, when it was split into the three new states of India, Pakistan and Ceylon. This was followed by other transfers of power to British, French, Dutch and Belgian colonies. Generally, independence came about by peaceful means, but in some cases the bonds with the former colonising power were only broken after long and bitter conflicts, with legacies of mistrust and suspicion. The French were particularly reluctant to relinquish control over their colonies, which they regarded in many ways as being part of the motherland. They were forced to do so after long nationalist wars, notably in Indo-China, 1945–54, and Algeria, 1954–62. In the ex-Belgian Congo, which became the Congo Republic in 1960, the situation after independence was so confused that the United Nations was invited to step in to restore order and provide a basis for unity. Some of the vestiges of empire remained in the form of loose unions such as the British Commonwealth and the French Union, but these do not hinder the exercise of full sovereignty by the member states.

THE NEW NATIONS

At the same time as these great empires have been breaking up, new countries on a continental scale have been growing in importance. The most important of these are the United States and the Soviet Union. Both of them participated significantly in the First World War, but after 1918 for different reasons they ceased to interest themselves in world affairs. In the case of the United States, a large section of opinion was opposed to what were referred to as 'foreign entanglements', and the country withdrew from active participation and became isolationist. The Soviet Union, heir to the Russian Empire after the revolution of 1917, was busy modernising and creating a structure of heavy industry in a country which until then had been relatively backward. Both of these countries were drawn in spite of themselves into the Second World War, and used their massive combined resources in alliance against Germany. After 1945, on account of the power they now wielded, they had responsibility thrust upon them, and each became the centre of opposing alliances. These were the North Atlantic Treaty Organisation (NATO) consisting of the United States, Canada and most of the Western European countries, and the Warsaw Pact of the Soviet Union and the countries with communist regimes in Eastern Europe.

Until the early 1950s these two power blocs dominated the world, but after this a new group of countries began to emerge which were 'non-aligned', that is to say not committed to either alliance. The hard core of these were the independent countries of Asia and Africa, notably India and Egypt, later to be joined by others. The great powers have wooed these countries with financial inducements and technical assistance, but for the most part the latter have found their intermediate position to be most advantageous.

In the last ten years the tremendous lead of the two 'super-powers' over the rest of the world has decreased, and new groups of countries are combining for reasons of economics and defence. Foremost among these is the European Economic Community, consisting of France, West Germany, Italy, Belgium, the Netherlands and Luxemburg. All of these countries, apart from Luxemburg, have been colonial powers in the past, and have a recent history of political and economic rivalry. It is significant that they have now submerged their differences so as to make a more effective unit in the present-day world.

THE ECONOMIC BACKGROUND

The important changes which have been occurring in the world political pattern owe a great deal to parallel changes in its economic structure. These have been no less fundamental than in the political sphere, and likewise reveal the decreased importance of Europe by comparison with other parts of the world. The period of the great European empires saw the growth of worldwide trade largely by and for Europeans. The major reason for the original expansion of Europe was so as to obtain those commodities in which the continent was deficient, notably tropical crops and certain minerals. At first these things were luxuries, but with increased production and improved transport many gained the character of necessities. Thus such things as coffee and tea which until the eighteenth century had been very expensive, became in the nineteenth national beverages in most European countries. By the late nineteenth century even those commodities which Europe had until then produced for herself had come to be imported in large quantities. Great Britain had traditionally been an exporter of wool, but her role was now reversed and she was forced to rely on imports in order to supply the expanding woollen industry of Yorkshire. Agriculture was neglected in favour of industry, and manufactured goods were then exported to pay for the primary imports. As a result of all this, by 1914 the greater part of the world had become one great trading area, with 'free trade' as the most popular, though not universally held, doctrine. Different areas had come to be characterised by a high degree of specialisation in production. The growing of cotton was concentrated in such areas as India, Egypt and the south of the United States, while its manufacture was no less concentrated in parts of Western Europe and North America. None of the great manufacturing regions produced even a small quantity of their raw materials, and conversely none of the producers were engaged in large-scale manufacture. Each was located hundreds or even thousands of miles away from the other. The whole of this system was held together by the ocean trade routes which spanned the globe and along which commodities were moved from producer to consumer.

The system which evolved in this way is, in its essentials, still the basis of world economic geography today. We in Britain continue to buy large quantities of Australian wool, and they in turn take our manufactured goods. But big changes have been taking place, and the system is far less clearcut than it was. If this were not so then Britain, the most significant of the trading nations, would not need to reconsider her economic policy to the extent she has been doing in the last few years. The fact that in recent years Britain has negotiated to join the European Economic Community shows that this country is no longer able to rely as before on the old system. Let us now consider briefly the main changes which have taken place, and judge their effects upon world economic geography.

ECONOMIC CHANGES

1. One of the most significant changes has been the economic advance of the producer countries. This has entailed an improvement in the methods of production and an increase in the standard of living in many of them. Many of them are also now manufacturing, thus competing with the exporting countries, who always paid for their purchases with industrial products. Such manufacture is usually started by using locally produced commodities which were formerly almost entirely exported. Most of the Indian cotton crop used to be sent to manufacturing regions such as Lancashire, and large quantities would be returned to India in the form of finished cotton goods. With the setting up of cotton mills in India itself, the dependence on foreign sources has therefore diminished. Local industries have the advantages of low labour costs and cheap raw materials, and so are able to undercut the prices of imported goods. This sort of industrial development is generally supported by the government, but loans and investments

from abroad are necessary to finance it. It helps to make these countries more self-sufficient, and so less dependent on world markets in primary goods.

2. At the same time the old industrial nations have made themselves in many ways more self-sufficient, and so less dependent upon the primary producers. This development dates from the First World War, when as a result of naval warfare trade was so disrupted that the belligerents were forced to rely increasingly on their own resources. Until then local supplies had been neglected in favour of low-cost imports. After 1945, as the result of further interruption of trade, destruction of resources and the general uncertainties of the world situation, there was a further tendency towards self-sufficiency in certain spheres. This has been accomplished in two ways:

a. An increase in the home production of primary commodities, both agricultural and mineral. In agriculture this has taken the form of turning over more and more land to farming, often land which became disused in the latter half of the nineteenth century. Yields have also been increased by improving seeds and stock. As a result of these things, Britain is now able to produce about 50 per cent of her own food supply, compared with 30 per cent before the Second World War. Europe's 'farm nations', Holland and Denmark, are now sending more and more of their temperate foodstuffs to the nearby highly industrialised nations. Likewise, Europe's mineral production is being augmented, and increasing amounts of the industrial minerals are coming from home or nearby sources. Symptomatic of this is the renewed interest in the possibility of getting tin from Cornwall, where mining virtually ceased half a century ago due to the ease with which the Malayan product could be imported.

b. The other development is the use of synthetics as substitutes for the natural material. Originally they were just stopgaps in time of emergency, but with advancing techniques many of them have proved so good and cheap that they are able to compete favourably with the real thing. Examples of such synthetics are artificial rubber, manmade fibres, plastics and chemical dyes; these are now made in large quantities in the industrial countries. The importance of these substances must, of course, depend upon the availability and price of the natural product. Thus, while it is possible to make synthetically both rubber and petroleum, only the former is produced in significant quantities, as petroleum is more readily available to the great consuming nations. The extent to which synthetics are relied upon will also vary from country to country, depending on natural resources and the circumstances of trade. The United States, for instance, produces no natural rubber but has abundant petroleum, and she uses this in order to make rubber synthetically. Great Britain has always imported rubber in large quantities from Malaya, and consequently she has had less interest in finding a substitute. (See page 40).

Such developments as have been outlined here are undeniably of great significance, and in time they may well radically alter the whole system of production as we know it today. However, as yet they must be kept in their proper perspective. International trade in primary commodities remains very great, and even with increased national self-sufficiency, the pattern is likely to remain similar into the foreseeable future.

3. Considerable economic significance is also attached to the rise of the new giant nations: the 'super-powers'. These countries carry out within their frontiers both primary production and manufacture, and thus have a high degree of self-sufficiency. The two outstanding examples of such countries are the United States and the Soviet Union.

TABLE I. *Comparative figures of extent, population and selected items of production for the USA, USSR and United Kingdom for* 1968

	USA	USSR	UNITED KINGDOM
AREA (in mill. sq. km)	9·4	22·4	0·24
POPULATION (in millions)	201·2	235·5	55·3
COAL PRODUCTION (in mill. tons)	500·5	440·0	166·7
CRUDE STEEL (in mill. tons)	121·9	106·2	26·3
PETROLEUM (in mill. tons)	526·0	310·0	0·1
ELECTRICAL ENERGY (in 1000 GWh)	1522·0	638·7	224·9

In area they are both vast by comparison with older industrial nations such as Great Britain. They both possess tremendous resources of all types, and their varied climates and soils facilitate a diversity of agriculture impossible in countries of smaller extent. The United States was first in the field, and by the 1890s had become the strongest industrial country in the world. By 1913 she was producing as much steel as all the major European producers put together. The USSR's development came later, and she did not really get under way industrially until the 1930s. During the last thirty years she has made great strides, and her economy in many sectors now bears comparison with that of the USA. (See Table 1.) Both of these countries have accomplished so much, not only because of their vast resources, but also because they are free-trade areas on a continental scale, and have large internal markets. Their external trade is far lower than one might think from a consideration of the national wealth, and the greater part of it is with adjacent countries.

They are both located in latitude between the Tropic of Cancer and the Arctic Circle – the USA stretching from 25° to 49° North, and the USSR from 36° to 77° North. Because of this they are able to produce tropical and subtropical crops only in limited areas, and the deficit has to be imported or substitutes obtained. They also have to import other materials for which the demand exceeds the supply, notably iron ore for the United States and food grains for the Soviet Union. Conversely there are often large surpluses, either of foodstuffs, or raw materials, or manufactured goods. What is available for export is nevertheless over and above that required on the home markets, rather than being a built-in feature of the economy as with those countries which 'export to live'.

4. Together with the tendency to greater self-sufficiency one should also mention the increased importance of regional trade, that is to say trade among adjacent or nearby countries. Not only is this helped by the ease of transport but such countries have also come to realise that they are often good markets for one another's goods. When they were colonial territories, the newer nations used to conduct their trade mainly with the colonising power, and had little contact with one another. With independence they have become more and more aware of one another's existence, and so are proceeding to strengthen their economic ties. In the case of the Commonwealth, the overall trade among member nations is not now increasing, but regional trade between members in the same area and with other nearby countries continues to increase.

The trade of Australia with New Zealand, for example, has grown rapidly in the last ten years, as also has that of Australia with parts of South-East Asia. At the same time the trade of Britain with Western Europe has grown more rapidly than has her trade with the Commonwealth.

It is this splitting up into islands of trade which has encouraged the formation of large economic blocs like the European Economic Community which has already been mentioned. The aim of such organisations is to remove as many restrictions as possible to the fullest possible economic integration so as to produce greater security and efficiency all round. They attempt to evolve common financial, industrial and agricultural policies which will be to their mutual benefit. In its total production, the EEC is now comparable to the superpowers themselves. Other areas endeavouring to combine in this way are the East European countries, which are grouped together with the USSR in 'Comecon', the Latin American countries, and the new African states. The advanced industrial nations have given considerable help to the less-developed ones within the framework of organisations of this sort. An even newer idea has been that of setting up a large economic unit covering all the Atlantic countries, that is to say broadly speaking those countries now grouped together for defence as the North Atlantic Treaty Organisation. This was strongly supported by the late President Kennedy, who looked forward to the time when these would be even more interdependent than they are at the present day.

This then is a brief picture of the background against which we shall study the economic geography of the world. It is a complex picture in which growth and decline are to be seen together in all aspects of human affairs. All these aspects, whether political, social or economic, are closely linked together, and understanding of one depends on understanding the others as well. The world is never static, and as old forms of organisation become unworkable, so new ones have to be evolved. It has been said that the Stock Exchange reflects the fortunes of all aspects of human affairs. In a different way this is no less true of economic geography, the study of which is an attempt to understand production and exchange, together with the factors which influence them over the surface of the earth. A fuller realisation of these things should make us the better able to grasp the significance of the great problems which are today facing all mankind.

Chapter 2

Organic Raw Materials 1 – The Physical Background and its Resources

ORGANIC products are those which derive from plants or animals. Some are obtained direct from the natural sources, but the great majority are now produced agriculturally. Early in man's economic development the natural products of hunting, collecting and fishing made up the sole sources of his food and clothing. With the beginning of agriculture, round about 6000 B.C., the human race took a significant step forward, and this was the first serious attempt by man to influence the sources of his supplies. Since these early beginnings, the selective breeding of plants and animals has become steadily more important, so that it now dominates the production of organic commodities. As dependence on unreliable natural sources has diminished, so supplies of necessary materials have become more assured.

There is still a range of products, such as vegetable waxes and oils, which can be obtained in sufficient quantities without the expense of systematic planting. This is also true of the furs and skins of many wild animals which thrive best in their natural environments. Although the bulk of the world's timber still comes from natural sources, the replacement of trees felled is becoming more and more necessary so as to ensure the continuity of supply.

The natural fauna and flora of any area are those which are best adapted to the prevailing natural conditions. These conditions can best be understood when separated into three groups:

I. THE LAND. The nature of the land surface, in respect of its height and relief has very considerable influence. Since temperatures decrease vertically by approximately 1·6° per 300 metres or roughly 3° F. per 1,000 feet, higher land will experience very different conditions from those of nearby lowlands. Slopes are very important to ensure good drainage, without which soils become acid and unfavourable to the growth of most plants. At the other extreme, very steep slopes result in thin, poor soils which are at least equally unfavourable to plant growth. The direction of slope is of great significance, as this determines the amount of insolation and its effectiveness. In the Northern Hemisphere, a south-facing slope will get more effective insolation than one facing north, and this simple fact has had great influence on the vegetation and agriculture of mountainous regions like the Alps.

2. THE CLIMATE. Climate is the sum total of weather conditions prevailing in any area. It is the result of the combined effects of temperature, precipitation, air pressure and associated elements such as humidity and wind force. Over large areas these combine to produce broadly similar conditions, such areas being referred to as 'climatic regions', which are repeated in many parts of the world. For instance, the climate characteristic of the British Isles and the adjacent parts of continental Europe, the Cool Temperate Western Maritime, is found in its essentials in three other parts of the world (see Appendix 1). Taking a world view, climate is the principal factor influencing the nature of the plant and animal life on the surface of the earth, and even the irregularities of the land surface are largely of importance because they themselves modify the local conditions of weather.

3. THE SOILS. Soil is the layer of decomposed mineral and organic material covering most of the land surface. The mineral parts result from the underlying geology, and the organic mostly from the overlying vegetation, and the nature and rate of its formation are determined by the climatic conditions. Extremes of any sort will have an adverse effect on the quality of the soils. Great heat and moisture, as found in the tropics, will rapidly decompose the humus, and so limit the amount of plant food available. Very heavy rainfall will contribute to eroding away the topsoil altogether and will impoverish what is left by leaching out minerals. In spite of these strong climatic effects, the nature of the local rocks can be of considerable importance, since they, after all, make up the greater part of the soil. Soils which develop on limestone are very rich in this mineral, and this is an important cause of the vegetation and agriculture which are likely to be found in such regions. Great Britain has a very diverse surface geology, and this has resulted in a wide variety of local soil types, each with its own

particular characteristics. Although most of the south of the country has soils which come into the general classification of 'grey-brown forest', the local differences are actually very considerable.

WORLD CLIMATES

It will be seen that while the nature of the land surface is a local factor, climate is a far more general one. The detailed causes of climatic differences throughout the world are very complex, and need not concern us here in the study of economic geography. To cut a long story short, the basic cause is the unequal heating of different parts of the earth's surface by the sun's rays. The equatorial regions get consistently the greatest amount of heat, the polar regions consistently the least, while in the intermediate areas – the mid-latitudes – it varies according to latitude and season. These differences affect the air pressure and its capacity to hold moisture, so in conjunction with the surface relief produce the rain, humidity, cloud cover and winds – in fact, all the elements of climate.

The ancient Greeks, who studied geography over 2,000 years ago, perceptively classified the world's climates into three types: torrid, temperate and frigid. A simplified classification along these lines into hot, temperate and cold zones, will be particularly useful for understanding the relationship between the climate and the distribution of plant and animal products. A more detailed classification of climates will be found in Appendix 1.

Hot

These climates are found mostly within the tropics, although they might extend beyond them in places. Average temperatures range between 21° and 32° C. (70° and 90° F.). In the wet areas near the Equator they remain remarkably constant, with annual variations generally less than 6·5° C. (10° F.). Near the Equator also there is heavy all-year rainfall, over 2,500 mm (roughly 100 inches) in many parts, but farther away it diminishes and becomes seasonal. Eventually it almost disappears in the hot dry areas, the extreme examples of which are deserts, classified as having less than 10 inches per annum. In such areas temperature variations, both seasonal and diurnal, become very great, and ranges of 65° C. (100° F.) in twenty-four hours are quite possible.

Cold

In most respects these are quite the opposite of the former climates. They are particularly well developed in the northern parts of North America and Eurasia, as well as in most high mountain areas throughout the world. Average temperatures are consistently very low, with the thermometer remaining below freezing point for many months of the year. During the summer very high temperatures can be experienced for limited periods. Precipitation and humidity are also low, much of the precipitation falling as snow.

Temperate

These climates are found in mid-latitudes, sandwiched between the other two. Although the term 'temperate' means moderate, it is in many ways deceptive, since there are considerable variations both in temperature and rainfall. Great temperature ranges are most common in the continental interiors, which warm up and cool rapidly, and have little cloud cover to modify the effects. The coastal areas, especially those facing the prevailing westerly winds on the western seaboards, have much smaller annual and diurnal ranges. The rainfall is considerable, although it varies from very heavy on coastal mountains, to light in rain-shadow areas.

THE NATURAL VEGETATION

The nature of the vegetation in any area is the result of the combined effects of the elements which make up its natural environment. There are three main types of natural vegetation: forest, grass and bush. Rainfall is the main determining factor, and forests are usually found in well-watered areas, grasses in moderate and bushes in areas where the rainfall is light or unreliable. The actual species which will be found in any area will be determined by temperature and other considerations.

There is little of the natural vegetation which is completely useless to man. Forests provide timber, together with resins and liquid extracts; grass is an important fodder for animals, and particular species such as reeds and esparto are useful as fibres, while many bushes are sources of perfumes, dyes and drugs. Yet, with certain important exceptions, the natural vegetation is of less general importance today than ever before. This is due to a number of causes including:

1. Its almost complete disappearance over large areas, especially in Europe, North America and South-East Asia.

2. Its replacement as a source of supply by the products of cultivated plants, the growth and yield of which can be more easily controlled. An example of this is the ploughing of grasslands in favour of the production of animal fodder crops.

3. The competition of other sources of supply, which are able to produce chemicals and other substances more cheaply. The by-products of coal and other materials now make good substitutes for vegetable substances.

Within this overall story of decline, the world's forests are an exception and are becoming more important economically. In spite of intensive use over the years, they are the largest and most important tracts of natural vegetation still existing. From the point of view of the nature of the species they can be divided into three groups – the tropical, the coniferous and the temperate.

Tropical Forests

These are densest near the Equator, where the 'global greenhouse' of the intertropical regions is most hot and wet. In the basins of Amazonia and the Congo, and the peninsulas and islands of South-East Asia, the trees are tall, close-packed and include a high proportion of valuable hardwoods. Farther out towards the tropics the forest becomes smaller, and much of it has been removed to make way for plantations. As a result of its difficult physical conditions, this fate has not befallen most of the high equatorial forest, and South-East Asia is the only intensively settled part of it.

Tropical hardwoods, notably teak, mahogany, ebony and greenheart, are highly prized in commerce. The most important producing area is South-East Asia, in particular Indonesia, Thailand and Burma. About 45 per cent of the world's tropical hardwood comes from these countries. The density of the forest, together with the large number of species, many of which are of little economic value, make the required woods difficult to secure and to transport. In Thailand and Burma elephants are used to move the wood, and it is floated down to the coast for shipment. The other important producing areas are Central America, West and East Africa and the western part of the Brazilian forest. In this latter area, one of the species is the balsa, a tropical giant which has one of the lightest of woods.

The main markets for this wood are the European and North American countries, where it is used for furniture and veneers, and for various internal and external purposes where its qualities of beauty and durability make it much sought after.

Coniferous Forests

Coniferous, or cone-bearing, trees are found naturally in many parts of the world, including areas of warm temperate climate and mountainous regions. However, in extent and economic significance, the most important are the northern coniferous forests which stretch in an irregular belt through North America between 45° and 65° North. After being interrupted by the North Atlantic, this belt is resumed in approximately the same latitudes through Scandinavia and the Soviet Union.

Although these forests are the world's most important single source of timber, producing about 45 per cent of the world total, their vast extent of 13·8 million sq. km (5·4 million square miles) has meant that large parts of them are almost untouched. The most important species are pine, fir, spruce and larch, and the timber obtained from them is softwood. Its uses are more varied than those of the tropical woods, and much of it is reduced to wood pulp, the raw material for paper, cardboard and a wide range of fibre boards used in packaging and in construction work. Increasingly it is providing the cellulose required for making many man-made fibres and plastics (p. 117). Softwood is also used in its original state in building, furniture and a great range of equipment. The following are the main producing areas:

NORTH AMERICA. This continent produces around 350 million cubic metres of coniferous wood per annum, this being one-third of the world's output. The United States is responsible for some two-thirds of this, the main lumbering regions being the West Coast, Alaska, the Appalachians and the South. Canada is the third world producer, and the Canadian forest is second in extent only to that of the Soviet Union. The provinces of Quebec, Ontario and British Columbia are the main producing areas. Throughout North America wood is used considerably in building construction since it is one of the cheapest and most abundant raw materials. With its large printing and publishing industry, the United States uses immense quantities of wood pulp, and much of this has to be imported from Canada. Large quantities of Canadian wood are also exported to Western Europe for similar purposes.

SCANDINAVIA. Sweden, Finland and Norway all have large forests, and coniferous trees make up the greater part of them (Fig. 2). In

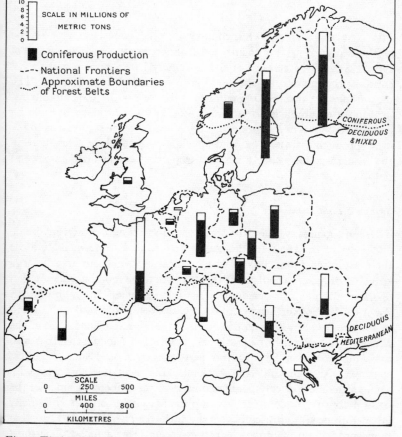

Fig. 2. Timber Production in the European Countries (excluding USSR). Most highland areas throughout the Continent contain large areas of coniferous forest

respect of timber production, these three countries occupy a similar position in relation to Europe to that of Canada to North America. Timber is one of their greatest resources, and its use is widespread for an immense range of goods. The craft of woodworking is very highly developed, especially in Sweden, and designs originating in that country are almost universally acclaimed. Much wood and pulp is exported, particularly to the great industrial countries of Western Europe.

THE SOVIET UNION. This country has the largest reserves in the world, and great parts of them are still almost untouched. Over much of central Siberia, as a result of the extremely harsh climate and frozen subsoils, the quantity of the wood is not matched by its quality. The most important area of exploitation is to the west of the Ural mountains, near to the economic heart of the country. It is used widely for building and to serve local needs, but does not enter into trade so much as in the other producing areas. The need for paper and cellulose is less than in the western countries, so a smaller proportion is converted into wood pulp.

Temperate Forests

These are generally found between the tropical and coniferous belts, and most of the trees are deciduous broadleaf. In intermediate areas these are often found mixed with tropical or coniferous trees. Large stretches of mixed woodland of this type are to be found at the junction of the coniferous and deciduous belts in the Soviet Union and North America. In the Northern Hemisphere, temperate forest alone is found in Europe between 45° and 60° North, in the United States east of the Mississippi, and much of north-east China and Manchuria. It is also to be found south of the equator in parts of extratropical South America, south-east Australia and New Zealand. This vegetation coincides with some of the most thickly populated parts of the globe, and much of the natural forest has completely disappeared. Great Britain and many other European countries have very little natural forest left, so that home production of timber is insufficient to meet demand. The most important woods economically are oak, ash, beech and elm, and these are much used for the making of furniture. Although workable woods, the lack of large reserves in most countries has diminished their usefulness.

Forest Plantation

As the best and most accessible reserves of timber have been steadily used up, so it has become necessary to start replenishing them by replanting. This is inevitably a long-term affair, since trees take many decades before they produce enough wood to be cut down economically. Conifers, which are by far the most rapid growers, take up to twenty years to mature sufficiently. This has prevented forestry from becoming a small-scale enterprise akin to agriculture, and in most cases it has therefore devolved on governments to initiate the necessary process of forest conservation and extension. The Scandinavians, for whom timber is of such importance, were among the first to start systematic tree planting, and the idea has now spread to many other countries. The most suitable trees for this purpose are conifers, since, besides growing rapidly, they have a wide climatic range and their wood is in great demand. Most wood-producing countries in the temperate and cold belts now practise forest conservation, and in many, such as New Zealand, thousands of acres of heathland have been planted. In Great Britain the Forestry Commission was set up in 1919, and it has been responsible for putting 600,000 hectares ($1\frac{1}{2}$ million acres) under woodland. Many mountainous areas in Wales and Scotland have been planted with saplings, and timber from this source is now contributing to home supplies. Recently it has been the Commission's policy to plant mixed conifer and broadleaf trees so as to diversify the timber available. The home production of wood in Great Britain has risen appreciably in recent years and is now approaching 4 million cubic metres annually. This is made up of almost equal quantities of coniferous and broadleaf wood.

As the great forests of the world become more and more depleted of natural trees, so plantation becomes more than ever vital. In this way, wood will become more in the nature of a crop like any other.

Other Forest Products

The number of products still obtained from forest trees continues to diminish, but there are still quite a number which can be obtained satisfactorily in this way. The most important of these are extracts from the bark or from the fruit of the trees.

RESIN. This is a general name for a number of viscous liquids found beneath the bark of trees. The most important is turpentine which comes from conifers, and is used as a solvent, and in the manufacture of paint, varnish, ink and paper. It is produced in the United States, Canada and many European countries.

WAX. Vegetable waxes are obtained from the berries and leaves of trees and bushes, and the tropical regions are the main suppliers. The most important is carnauba wax from the leaves of the carnauba palm. It is used in the making of polishes and waxed papers, and the main supplier is north-east Brazil.

OILS AND GUMS. The tropical trees are rich in oils, the most economically important being those from the palm, camphor and eucalyptus. Palm oil is in such great demand now that more and more of it is coming from plantations (see Chapter 3). Gum arabic, the most important constituent of adhesives, is also obtained from a species of palm.

Other important extracts are those from the cinchona tree, the bark of which yields *quinine* and quebracho wood from which *tannin* is obtained. *Brazil nuts* come from a tree native to the tropical forests of South America, and are one of Brazil's most characteristic exports.

WILD ANIMALS

In past times wild animals were a principal source of man's food and raw materials, but today they are only of significance for providing a limited number of items. Their coats are still used extensively for clothing, rugs and upholstery. *Furs* are of special significance, and the best of these are from those animals whose natural habitats are in the cold lands of the coniferous and tundra belts. These include beaver, bear, musk ox, silver fox, chinchilla, ermine, sable, musquash, otter and mink. Many of these furs are extremely costly and much sought after, while others are very common, and are used widely for clothing in the colder lands. The most important producing regions are the northern parts of North America and Eurasia. Here the animals are trapped in large numbers, and are also traded from native people such as the Eskimo of northern Canada. During the present century fur farming has become increasingly widespread, especially for valuable animals such as mink, chinchilla, sable and ermine. This has the advantage of making supplies more regular, and of enabling fur to be produced in many more countries than would otherwise be possible. It is being undertaken on a large scale in Canada, the USA, the USSR and many European countries.

While by far the greatest supplies of *hides and skins* come from domesticated animals, an important contribution is made by such mammals as the seal and walrus native to the coastal waters of northern seas. Many tropical animals have long been hunted for their hides, but the most prized have become rarer, and are now being protected by the provision of reserves. *Animal extracts* such as musk, castor, civet and ambergris are used in perfumes, and those from insects such as cochineal and kermes in dyes. Animal and other organic dyes, however, are now being replaced to a large extent by synthetic substances (see p. 117). *Bone* has considerable uses in the making of many utensils and in production of glue, oils, fertiliser and chemicals. The greater part of the world's supplies again comes from domestic animals, but *ivory* comes almost entirely from the tusks of elephants. The waters off East and South-East Asia are very rich in *shells*, *coral* and *sponges*. In this area also are *pearl*-producing oysters, and in Japan, 'cultured' pearls are produced by artificially inducing them.

An important oil is obtained from whales, the main hunting grounds for which are now in the Antarctic region. Modern factory ships dispose of the whale at sea, and most of it is used up in producing sperm oil, whale oil, bone and fertiliser. Also of importance is cod-liver oil used widely for medicinal purposes.

STUDENT WORK

1. Define the precise meanings of the following terms which have been used in this chapter: PRECIPITATION; ATMOSPHERIC HUMIDITY; INSOLATION; DIURNAL; HUMUS; LEACHING. (This can be made

the start of a geographical vocabulary in which the meanings of terms used in this course can be noted down.)

2. What are the geographical factors responsible for making tropical hardwoods much more expensive than coniferous softwoods?

3. With the aid of a sketch map, explain the factors which particularly favour the exploitation of coniferous wood in south-east Canada.

4. Draw bar graphs to show the following statistics for roundwood production in North America in 1962:

Country	Total production	Coniferous only
	(in million cubic metres)	
CANADA	92·8	83·1
COSTA RICA	1·7	–
HONDURAS	3·3	2·2
MEXICO	4·3	3·0
USA	293·2	209·0

Describe and comment on the information revealed by your graphs, and compare them with the most recent figures available to you. (Consult Appendix 3 for information on drawing graphs.)

5. Compare and contrast the timber production of the United Kingdom, Italy and Finland, explaining the differences you find.

6. In what ways do the natural conditions of the coniferous forests limit the extent of their development?

7. Why is wood of such great economic significance in the Scandinavian countries?

8. Explain why the USSR is so important as a producer of furs.

Chapter 3

Organic Raw Materials 2 – The Agricultural Background and its Resources

APART from the all-important exceptions already considered, the organic raw materials used in industry are now overwhelmingly products of agriculture. Man has therefore become an active agent in natural processes, since it is he who decides where he will select to produce his varied needs. However, it is not basically his decision whether they will succeed or not, and the most important task confronting him is to decide aright where the best conditions for his purposes are to be found.

There are many clues to help in such judgments, particularly a climatic similarity to areas already producing a commodity, or the presence of wild species. The history of farming has been one of trial and error, since the only way to determine what is most suitable to any area is by experiment. The present world pattern of agriculture represents the stage that has now been reached in this process of trial and error, and the factor that has had the greatest overall influence on it is undoubtedly climate.

Although the best conditions for individual plants and animals are in each case different, particular groups are well suited to broadly similar ones. These groups are closely related to the climatic regions considered in the previous chapter, except that the cold zone has virtually no agriculture at all. Between the tropical and temperate belts an intermediate subtropical region can be distinguished with its own individual set of products. The main characteristics of the farming of each of the three belts, are discussed below, primarily from the point of view of those materials used industrially.

TROPICAL

Agriculture within the tropics is concerned mainly with vegetable products, and domesticated animals are of little importance except where there is considerable climatic modification on account of altitude.

There is a marked contrast between primitive subsistence agriculture and the plantations which export the bulk of their crops. The most important products entering into commerce are rubber, vegetable oils, spices, fibres and fruit, together with beverages like coffee, cocoa and tea.

TEMPERATE

This type of agriculture is most highly developed in mid-latitudes between 40° and 60° North in Europe, the USSR, North America and the Far East. It is also characteristic of those parts of the southern continents outside the tropics. Various grasses, both for animal fodder and as cereals for human consumption, play a big part in the agriculture. The relative importance of the two uses changes with both the physical and the economic conditions. Animals are of especial importance in the cool maritime localities where the climate is very well suited to them, but they play at least a significant part in farming throughout most of the belt. The most numerous animals are cattle, sheep, pigs and poultry. Cereals and fruit are best grown in the more continental and southerly regions respectively, but where there are large urban populations, the whole farming system will be tailored to their needs. Their requirements of fresh pastoral produce, vegetables and fruit result in a highly specialised farming which owes as much to the economic as to the physical conditions.

SUBTROPICAL

This belt is found between the Tropic of Cancer and approximately 40° North, and similar conditions are found to a more limited extent in the southern hemisphere. Its natural conditions are in many ways a combination of those of the other two, and its agricultural diversity reveals this clearly. As in the tropics, vegetable products are most important, although animal farming is on the increase. The cultivation of fibres, notably cotton, silk, sisal and grasses is very characteristic, as also is that of cane sugar and fruit.

In spite of the overall suitability of the climatic conditions in each of these belts for a wide range of products, the actual production of particular commodities is in all cases much more limited. A glance at a map showing world production of, say rubber, will demonstrate this fact (Fig. 8). The exact locality of production is the result of the operation of a number of factors, in particular the following:

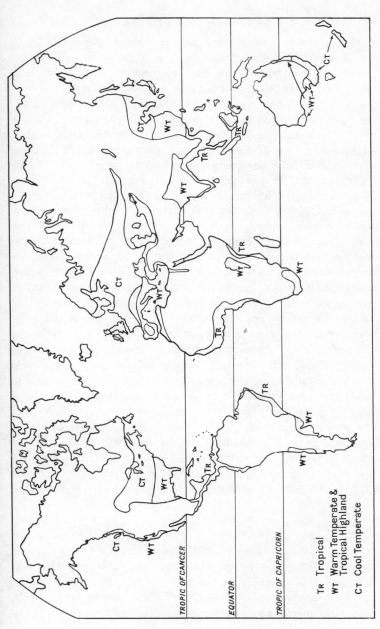

Fig. 3. The World. Major Agricultural Regions and Types

Tr Tropical

Wt Warm Temperate &
    Tropical Highland

Ct Cool Temperate

TROPIC OF CANCER

EQUATOR

TROPIC OF CAPRICORN

1. The suitability of the local physical conditions. This is not only a matter of climate but also of the soils, aspect and drainage. The soil should be the right type for the crop, and many agricultural projects have failed because this was not the case.

2. An adequate labour supply, both willing and able to work on the farm or plantation. A local labour supply will be well adapted to the climate, and will cost less than would bringing in workers from outside. If the particular type of commodity is already produced in the area, this may be a further inducement to development.

3. Political stability is essential, since without it the whole business could be in danger. Until the Second World War the great importing nations of Europe had attempted to ensure such stability by making the producing areas into colonies or protectorates. Since practically all these territories have now achieved their independence, the sources are no longer under the control of the consumers. Considerations such as the stability, friendliness and political opinions of the new governments now influence the consuming nations in deciding which of their sources of supply are likely to prove most reliable. The ideal situation – for the consumer – is when consumption and production are in the same country, but there is no nation on earth near to being able to do this.

4. Transport must be sufficient through all stages in the movement of the commodities. Since water transport remains the cheapest and most efficient means of moving raw materials over long distances, nearness to the sea or a large waterway is a great advantage. Because of the large quantity of goods being moved in certain areas, these routes have become very important, and proximity to them will cut time and costs.

As we now go on to consider the world production of industrial raw materials, these four factors should be kept in mind. The materials of organic origin will be considered in two major groups: (1) natural fibres; and (2) liquids, together with general products.

NATURAL FIBRES

Fibres can be classified into the textile group, which will bind together and so can be spun and woven into cloth, and the others, which do not have this quality and are used as they are. The textile fibres, as the raw material for clothing and a variety of fabrics, are by far the most important, the main ones being wool, cotton, linen and silk.

Wool

Most of the world's supplies of wool come from sheep, but small quantities of particular types come from other animals, notably goats and the llama and alpaca of South America. Wool is a strong hair-like substance, and its binding quality is due to its coating of minute scales. Spinning is also helped by the elasticity and the length of the fibres, which average about 125 mm (5 inches) in merino wool.

Wool is the most important local textile fibre available in mid-latitudes. Sheep, being adversely affected by very cold or very hot weather, do best in such areas. For best results the ground underfoot should be dry, and the rainfall as low as is compatible with ensuring an adequate water supply. The best wool-producing animal is the merino, a Spanish breed, and this, together with some English crossbreeds, accounts for about three-quarters of the world's supply.

PRODUCING REGIONS. With an output of 800,000 tons, 30 per cent of the world total, Australia is by far the most important producer. The country's 150 million sheep are reared mainly in the eastern states of Queensland, New South Wales and Victoria, and there is an especial concentration in the Murray–Darling basin. Here the temperatures are cooler than farther north, and these combined with the natural temperate grassland, ample space and low rainfall make a very suitable environment for the heavy-coated merino. The problem of water supply is serious in the drier districts, but this has been much aided by the discovery of large artesian sources. All these things would not necessarily in themselves have given rise to sheep rearing, were it not for the great demand for the product. This was for long monopolised by the British market, but today Australian wool is sent to a large number of other industrial countries.

In the other big Southern Hemisphere producers – New Zealand, South Africa and Argentina – the rearing areas have many physical similarities to those of Australia, the four of them together being responsible for 55 per cent of total world production.

Most of the temperate countries of the Northern Hemisphere are also wool producers, the two most important being the USA and the USSR. The latter country, with 400,000 tons, comes second to Australia. The

countries of Western Europe together account for 160,000 tons, half as
much again as the USA and 6 per cent of the world total. Between
them Great Britain and Spain produce nearly two-thirds of this,

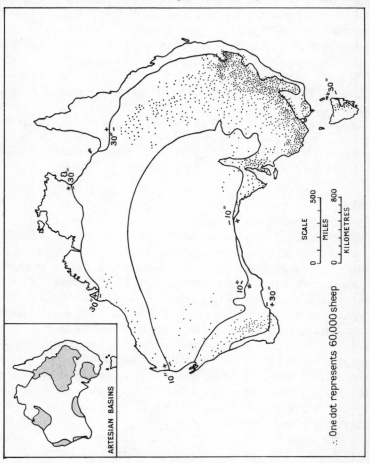

Fig. 4. The Distribution of Sheep in Australia. Together with Isohyets
for 250 mm (10 inches) and 750 mm (30 inches). Artesian basins (inset)

although the natural conditions of these two countries are very different.
In the latter country the main producing region is the hot Meseta with
less than 625 mm (25 inches) rainfall and a semi-continental temperature

range. By contrast, in Britain the sheep areas are mainly the western uplands, with cool to cold temperatures and usually over 1,000 mm rainfall (40 inches) – frequently far more.

Although Britain is Europe's main wool producer, she is also the world's main importer of raw wool. Her main supplies are the four countries of the Southern Hemisphere, and in particular Australia. The other western European countries are also big importers, mainly from the same sources.

Cotton

Raw cotton is a white fibrous material forming a 'boll' to protect the seeds of a species of grass known as *Gossypium*. The most important varieties used industrially for textiles are the following:

1. Indian cotton (*Gossypium herbaceum*). This is a short staple variety grown extensively today in India and parts of Africa.

2. American cotton (*Gossypium hirsutum*). Also short staple, this variety makes up the greater part of United States production.

3. Sea Island cotton (*Gossypium barbadense*). This is a long staple variety which is native to the southern United States. It is used for high quality cotton goods, and is grown in many countries, in particular Egypt.

Cotton is planted annually, and requires a long growing season with at least 200 days frost-free. There must be a good supply of moisture, and the best rainfall range is between 500 and 1,000 mm (20 and 40 inches), with spring and summer dominance. It also needs plenty of sunshine and dry weather for picking. This makes the plant most suited to the subtropical belt, but it is further confined by the need for rich well-drained soils. For tending and picking the crop a large labour force is necessary, although with increased mechanisation this is less true than formerly. The 'ginning' or separating out of the fibre from the seeds and waste is done at the producing end, and this also needs adequate labour.

WORLD PRODUCTION. The leading producer is now the Soviet Union which grows over 2 million tons per annum, about one-fifth of the world's crop. Soviet output has more than doubled since the late 1940s, and in 1967 she overtook the United States. The main producing regions

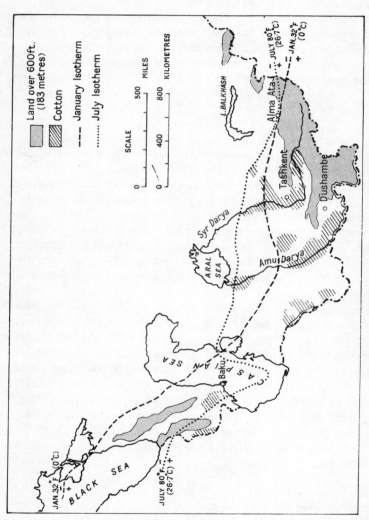

Fig. 5. Cotton Growing Areas of the Soviet Union

are in Central Asia, 70 per cent coming from Uzbekistan alone. Here the hot, dry and sunny climate together with long frost-free summers makes it most suitable, but water has to be obtained by irrigation since rainfall is almost everywhere less than 500 mm (20 inches), and in most places below 400 mm (16 inches). The largest schemes are connected with the Amu Darya and Syr Darya rivers and these are bringing more of the otherwise inhospitable areas into cultivation. In European Russia only Transcaucasia produces cotton, but it grows only about 5 per cent of the country's total crop. Farther north in European Russia cotton growing has been tried, but has not been a success.

The United States was for a century and a half the most important source of the world's cotton, but in the last two decades its production has been halved. After the Second World War it was responsible for some 40 per cent of the world output, but now produces only 15 per cent of it. This dramatic change has been brought about by a number of factors including the competition of synthetic fibres, decline in exports and troubles in the growing area itself.

The main cotton-producing region of the country lies south of 37° North, and east of 100° West (Fig. 6). Until the early nineteenth

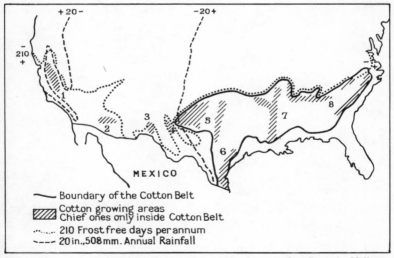

Fig. 6. Cotton in the United States. *Key to Numbers:* 1. San Joaquin Valley. 2. Gila Basin. 3. Rio Grande Valley. 4. Pecos Valley. 5. West Texas. 6. Gulf Coast. 7. Mississippi Valley. 8. Appalachian Fringes

century all the plantations were along the east coast in Georgia and the Carolinas, in the area where the Sea Island variety grows wild. Since that time the Cotton Belt has extended steadily westwards, and the eastern areas have declined in importance. This has been due to soil exhaustion, inferior climate and the ravages of an insect pest known as the boll weevil in the earlier part of this century. Texas is now the most important producing state, accounting for over half the crop, and more recently cultivation has jumped the Rocky Mountain barrier to California (10 per cent) and other parts of the West.

In all these western areas, including much of Texas, the annual rainfall is below that generally considered as a necessary minimum, but

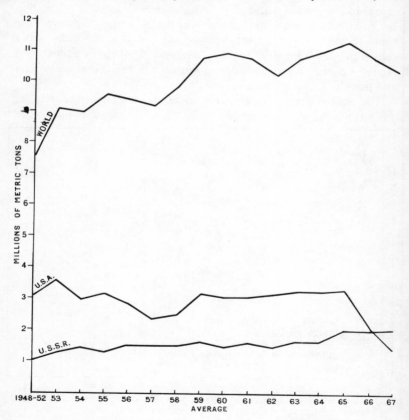

Fig. 7. Cotton Production. USA, USSR and World Total

irrigation and improved varieties have come to the rescue. Once the water supply could be ensured in this way, the general dryness became a positive advantage, since it discouraged the boll weevil and aided ripening and harvesting. This is an example of the way in which the breaking down of one geographical barrier has opened the way to a whole new range of possibilities.

The other most important world producers are China, India and Pakistan. Cotton growing has taken place in them for thousands of years and the crop is of great significance in their economies both for domestic use and for exporting. Another significant producing region is Latin America, and Brazil and Mexico between them account for over a million tons per annum.

Some of the most spectacular recent developments have in fact occurred in smaller producing countries, as can be judged from the table below.

TABLE 2. *Selected production of cotton.*

	1,000s metric tons		
	1956	1963	1968
SPAIN	29	96	71
SYRIA	70	153	159
IRAN	54	115	160
GUATEMALA	7	65	74
SUDAN	87	159	184

In Sudan production has doubled during the last decade to its present 180,000 tons. The greater part of the country has rainfall which is both too little and too unreliable for successfully growing the crop, and irrigation from the Nile and its tributaries is essential. Cotton is grown on the lands irrigated by the Sennar Dam on the Blue Nile, and also in the Gezira district south of Khartoum and its Managil extension brought into production in 1962. Now half a million hectares (1·2 million acres) are under the crop, which is mostly of a high quality long staple variety flourishing in the dry, sunny conditions. Sudan is now the world's major producer of extra long staple cotton (over 30 mm or $1\frac{1}{4}$ inches).

COTTON CONSUMPTION. The greatest consumers of raw cotton are the textile industries of the great industrial nations. The United States, Europe, the USSR and Japan among them use 60 per cent of world production, although themselves producing only 44 per cent. Virtually all this latter is produced in the USA and the USSR, both of whom are self-sufficient as regards cotton. The main supplies for the European countries come from the USA, the Indian subcontinent and Africa. Consumption in the industrial countries is, however, expanding far more slowly than in the world as a whole, and the surplus is going to feed the new industries in the producer countries themselves. The only exception to this is Japan which, though not itself a producer, is expanding its consumption.

Flax

Flax, the raw material of linen, is a tall grass which grows to two or three feet in height. As a vegetable textile fibre, it comes next in importance to cotton. The length of the individual fibres is from 30 to 45 mm ($1\frac{1}{4}$ to $1\frac{3}{4}$ inches), and they are separated from the stem of the plant by 'retting', that is steeping it in water for a period of time so as to enable the waste matter to be removed. Only the longest fibres are used in linen manufacture, the shorter ones being used to make cord and high quality paper.

Flax grows best in the cool temperate regions, almost the entire world output coming from Europe and the USSR. The latter country with an annual production of nearly 5 million metric tons accounts for two-thirds of the total world output. The highest quality fibre is from the more humid regions, particularly Belgium, Northern France and Northern Ireland. Most of the producing countries have their own established linen industries, so international trade is on a restricted scale.

Silk

As an animal fibre, silk comes next in importance to wool, but its production is much more localised, and its use more limited. Silk is the fine thread wound out by a species of caterpillar to protect its chrysalis. When the silkworm has covered itself the spinners unwind it, at the same time twisting it with strands from a number of others to form a stronger thread.

As the worm eats only the leaves of the mulberry bush, rearing is confined to regions suitable to this plant. Mulberry does best in areas with long hot summers, high humidity and moderate to heavy rainfall. As one would expect the worms themselves thrive in similar conditions, but as they can be kept indoors the climate is of less direct influence.

About 90 per cent of the world's silk supply comes from the warm temperate regions of South-East Asia, particularly China and Japan, and to a smaller extent India. In this latter country a coarse wild silk called tussore is of some commercial importance. Not only are the natural conditions of South-East Asia most suitable but the large populations also provide an adequate supply of workers skilled in the intricacies of silk production. Much of the silk is woven locally as it has been for thousands of years, but large quantities are exported to the North Atlantic countries to feed their weaving industries.

There is some local production in southern Europe, particularly in northern Italy. The Rhône valley of south-east France was once of importance, but this has steadily declined.

Other Vegetable Fibres

There are a large number of other vegetable fibres which are of some importance, but their uses are either confined to particular areas or to specialised purposes.

JUTE. This is in many ways a tropical equivalent to flax, but it produces a material which is much rougher and is generally used for sacking. It is a tall grass from 2 to 4 metres (roughly 5–15 feet) in height, and as in the case of flax the fibres are separated from the vegetable pulp by retting. The plant requires a hot growing season of three to four months with heavy rainfall, together with a rich alluvial soil. The bulk of world production is concentrated into the lower Ganges and its delta, an area which is shared between India and Pakistan. Until quite recently the greater part of the crop was exported, but ever larger quantities are now remaining in the producing area where many large mills cope with its spinning and weaving. Nearly a half of all exports go to Europe (including the USSR) and the largest single importer is Great Britain whose share, however, has been decreasing in recent years. Dundee is the most notable British importing centre and has been for over a hundred years the centre of a large jute industry.

HEMP. As a plant this is very similar to jute, and it produces a very coarse material used for ropes and canvas. Unlike jute, its climatic range is very wide, including the tropical and temperate regions. Most is produced in the latter area, the main countries being the USSR, Yugoslavia and Italy.

Another rope fibre of importance is *sisal* obtained from the leaves of a plant similar to the agave, which also yields fibre in certain circumstances. It is native to tropical countries, and grows best where conditions are constantly warm. Tanzania and Indonesia are the two main producers. *Coir* from coconuts and *pineapple fibre* are two other tropical fibres with similar uses. There are also many other so-called 'hemps' which are different from true hemp, though producing a similar product. Notable among them is *manilla hemp* from the leaves of a tree similar to the banana. In a different category comes *esparto*, a tall grass from North Africa, used principally for rope and paper.

ORGANIC FLUIDS

Those commodities which in their natural state are either fluid or semi-fluid make up another important group. They are found mostly in the form of oils, fats, gums, resins and waxes, and they come both from plants and from animals. For industrial use, they are combined with other substances to form such things as soaps, detergents, paint, varnish, polish, inks, linoleum and perfume (see Chapter 7). A large number of these fluids are required only in very small quantities, and can still be obtained in adequate quantities from wild plants and animals. Those which are produced agriculturally are either needed in very large quantities, like the major vegetable oils, or, like cotton seed, are obtained as by-products. The vegetable products are of the greatest diversity and industrial importance, and one of these, rubber, is in a class on its own.

Rubber

During the course of the present century, *rubber* has become one of the most vital of all industrial commodities. Its most significant use is for the tyres of motor vehicles and for rubber tubing, but when hardened through the addition of sulphur and other chemicals, it makes substances which can be used for a large number of utensils and fittings.

Rubber is made from a white liquid called latex, a mixture of resins and hydrocarbons, found beneath the bark of a certain species of tropical tree. There are many varieties of such trees, including the Guayule, native to Central America, but today the most widespread latex-yielding tree is *Hevea braziliensis*. Although a native to the forests of Amazonia, this is now found in plantations throughout the equatorial regions of the world.

It was the invention of the motor vehicle at the end of the last century which changed the fortunes of rubber, and made it one of the most irreplaceable of all vegetable products. Until then it had been used for a variety of purposes, especially for waterproofing. About 98 per cent of the world's supplies came from the Brazilian forest, all being collected from the wild forest trees. Most of it was bought from Indians who coagulated the liquid over smoke fires, making a variable and generally unsatisfactory product. Besides, this indiscriminate tapping was doing permanent harm to the trees, and the increasing demand was fast out-running Brazil's limited capacity to supply.

This situation was completely changed by the experimental introduction of hevea trees into the British colony of Ceylon in 1877, and into other South-East Asian countries a few years later. It took to this region better than anyone had dared to hope, and such has been the development of the industry that the region now produces 90 per cent of the world's supplies.

The hevea tree is confined to regions having equatorial climates, and it also does best on well-drained land, below 300 metres (nearly 1,000 feet) in height, where the soils are deep and rich. Poor drainage, causing prolonged inundation, results in a thin latex.

Throughout the present century the proportion of wild rubber in commerce has declined steadily, and now it makes up no more than a small fraction of the total. Practically all the world's supplies are at present from plantations. A plantation is a farm on which is grown one or more of the tropical products. It may be owned either by an individual or by a company, and varies in size correspondingly. Until quite recently the majority of tropical plantations were wholly or partly owned by foreign companies, generally European or North American, which provided the capital and the trained personnel. Today, local participation in all stages of production is becoming increasingly common, and in some places foreign interests have been bought up.

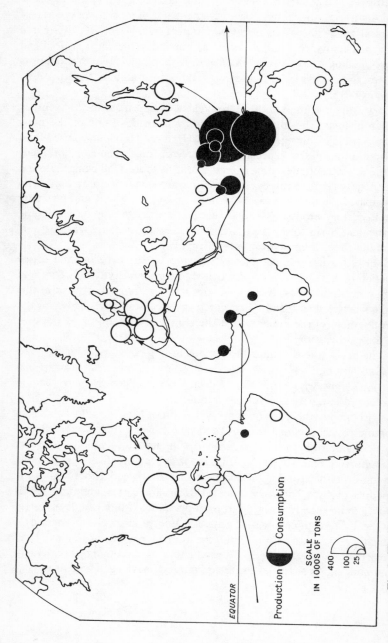

Fig. 8. World Production and Consumption of Natural Rubber. Arrows denote main lines of international trade

Before rubber trees can be planted the natural forest cover has to be removed by burning; this procedure provides potash to enrich the soils. The trees are grown from seed, and planted out together according to their age. They are first tapped when five years old, but do not reach maximum yield until some years later. Tapping is carefully regulated to ensure that the trees are not permanently impaired. The liquid oozes out from a slit cut in the bark, and on collection is coagulated by heating and the addition of acetic acid. After rolling and drying, it is ready to be exported to the consuming countries. This preparation of the rubber is generally carried out on the plantations, though some is exported in its liquid form.

WORLD PRODUCTION. World production of natural rubber has increased steadily from 2 million tons in 1960 to 2·5 million in 1968. Malaysia with 750,000 tons per annum is the world's largest producer. The greater part of this is from Malaya itself, and only about 50,000 tons originates in the eastern territories of Sabah and Sarawak. Malaysia is followed closely by the neighbouring state of Indonesia with 800,000 tons. This represents a considerable increase over the early 1960s when domestic and foreign difficulties contributed to a decrease in output. Today Malaysia and Indonesia together produce some 70 per cent of the world's supplies.

Rubber growing in Malaya is concentrated on the western side of the peninsula where the natural conditions are most favourable (Fig. 9). About 55 per cent of the 1·4 million hectares (3½ million acres) under rubber consists of large estates, mostly foreign owned; the remainder is in smallholdings belonging to native Malays. The greater part of the rubber is exported to the large industrial countries via the ports of Singapore, Port Swettenham and Penang.

Of the one-third of world output not originating in either Malaysia or Indonesia, the greater part comes from the adjacent countries of Thailand, Vietnam, Cambodia and Ceylon. This last country was the first in which plantation rubber was tried, but it now produces only one-seventh as much as Malaysia. Thailand, the third world producer, has increased its output considerably in recent years, while the countries of Indo-China have been seriously affected by the war in Vietnam. Similarly the output of Nigeria, formerly the most important African producer, has been hit by the civil war, and Liberia has now overtaken her. The share of Africa in the world production has gone up considerably in the last twenty years – from 2·5 per cent in 1948 to 6 per cent in 1968.

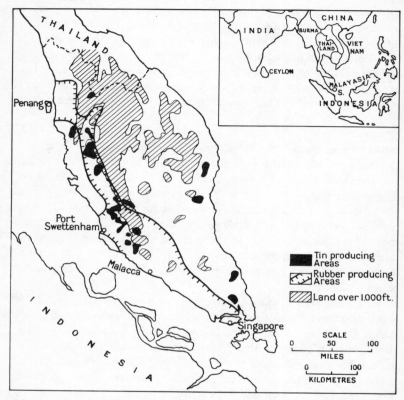

Fig. 9. Rubber and Tin in Malaya. (Inset shows location of Malaysia in relation to the other countries of South-East Asia)

TRENDS IN WORLD PRODUCTION. During the thirteen years from 1948 to 1962 the world production of rubber increased by 25 per cent from 1·5 million tons to 2·1 million tons. However, in 1948 production was still at quite a low level in South-East Asia as a result of war damage and trade disruption. Between 1954 and 1962 world production remained almost stable at a time when industries using rubber – for example, motor vehicles – have been rapidly increasing output. In the last few years output has once more started to increase but on nothing like the scale of these manufacturing industries. This situation can be explained by reference to a number of factors:

1. Synthetic rubber. This chemical substitute has been made for many years, but not until after 1945 did its quality make it an effective competitor with real rubber. In 1948 it accounted for 20 per cent of all the rubber produced, while by 1964 it had risen to over 50 per cent and by 1968 to over 60 per cent. Most of the production of synthetic is carried out in the great consumer countries, and the United States alone produces one-half of the world output.

2. Various types of plastic materials are now replacing the rubber derivatives like vulcanite and ebonite over a wide range of manufactures.

3. As a result of higher wages and other factors in the producing countries, the cost of natural rubber has risen, and its attractiveness for many purposes has therefore decreased.

4. With the gaining of political independence, many of the producer countries have experienced both internal and international difficulties. This has discouraged the investment of capital, and has encouraged foreign interests to look elsewhere for their raw materials.

Oils and Fats

The difference between an oil and a fat is one of degree, and depends upon the temperature at which it becomes solid. Palm oil is a liquid when pressed from the fruit of the West African oil palm, but it will have solidified when it is imported into Great Britain. These products are obtained both from plants and from animals, and we will consider the main sources of each.

VEGETABLE. There is a large number of commercially useful vegetable oils, each having its own individual characteristics. Certain oils, such as linseed and sunflower seed, harden with evaporation, and are therefore used for paints, varnish and ink. In contrast to these drying oils are the non-drying oils, such as groundnut and castor oil, which are used in foodstuffs, chemical and medical preparations. Between these two are the semi-drying oils and fats, particularly the oil of the palm, cotton-seed, corn, coconut and sesamum, and soya bean, all of which are used for soaps, candles and edible purposes.

Although oil-yielding plants are found over a wide climatic range, the tropical and subtropical belts are the most prolific sources. The oil and coconut palms are native to the equatorial lowlands, and the tropics and subtropics favour annual plants like cotton and groundnuts. In many cases the main purpose in growing is to obtain some other material, and oil is extracted as a by-product. An example of this is cotton, the seeds of which are separated from the fibre in the ginning process, so that cottonseed oil comes from almost the same sources as does cotton fibre.

PALM OIL is extracted from both the fruit and the kernel of the oil palm, and is one of the most important of industrial oils. The oil from the fruit is crushed out in the producing regions, but the kernels are usually exported as they are. The tree, which can attain a height of nearly 20 metres (65 feet) is a native to West Africa. Like the hevea it is confined to equatorial areas, doing best where the soils are deep and rich.

West Africa is the most important producing region, and it accounts for 63 per cent of the world's output (Fig. 10). Much still comes from

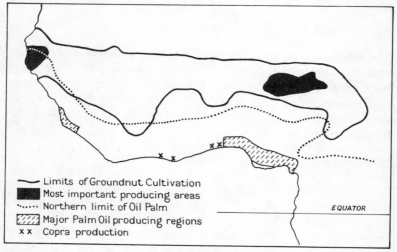

Fig. 10. West Africa. Production of Vegetable Oils

forest trees, but ever-increasing quantities are from plantations, the changeover being similar to that of rubber half a century ago. Nigeria has the largest output, although its total 840,000 tons in 1963 declined to 543,000 tons in 1968 on account of the civil war. In the latter year this was 30 per cent of the world total compared to 40 per cent in 1963. The country's production is made up of almost equal quantities of oil and kernels. Other important producers in this area are the Congo Republic, Ivory Coast and Sierra Leone.

The second major producing region is the Far East, in particular Malaysia and Indonesia, which between them account for about 14 per cent of world production. In this area all the oil comes from plantations, and output is rapidly increasing; in Malaysia it has doubled over the last ten years.

Another semi-drying oil of a similar sort is that obtained from the coconut palm. The need for a large and constant water supply confines it to tropical coasts. It is found particularly in India and South-East Asia, but has now spread to Africa. The oil comes from the fleshy part of the nut which is dried and exported as copra.

Like most of the other vegetable oils, these are exported in large quantities to the industrial countries, the largest consumers being those of Western Europe.

Linseed oil is the oil which is extracted from the seeds of the flax plant, and is used for paints, varnish, linoleum and other floorings. About three-quarters of the world's acreage of flax is sown with a view to obtaining this oil. Unlike cotton, the oil is not a by-product of the fibre production, since the fibres of the best oil-yielding plants are generally very poor in quality. The best oil is from the warm temperate regions, the most important being that of the New World which accounts for a half of the world total of around 3 million tons per annum. The world's largest sources are the United States and Argentina which between them account for three-quarters of New World output. The other most important producer is the USSR which has increased its output considerably in recent years.

Formerly the seeds were exported to be crushed out in the consuming countries, but nowadays increasing quantities of the oil are being treated in the places where they are produced. The largest oil exporter is Argentina, which alone is responsible for about four-fifths of all the oil entering international trade. All the other large producers also export, and the main market is Western Europe where the demand is great, but the local production very small.

ANIMAL OILS AND FATS come almost entirely from the temperate regions, and especially from those which specialise in meat production. The most important countries are Australia, New Zealand, Argentina and the USA and USSR. The main animals used for this purpose are cattle, sheep and pigs. Fat taken from cattle and sheep is known as tallow, and that from pigs as lard. Besides being used for culinary purposes, these fats are used in the manufacture of soaps, candles and lubricants. Gelatine from the bones is a purer substance, and isinglass made from this is used in clarifying liquids. The range of animal oils is much smaller than those of vegetable origin, and the total production is smaller.

Allied to these are FISH OILS which have been treated on page 21.

OTHER COMMODITIES

A large number of other agricultural products must be mentioned which are so diverse in character that they cannot be classified into a single group.

Vegetable

TOBACCO is the large leaf of an annual plant, 1 metre (3–4 feet) in height. It was introduced into Europe from North America in the seventeenth century, and the British colonies, later the United States, became the main supplier. The country has retained this position to the present day, and accounts for over a quarter of all tobacco entering world trade. Tobacco growing is mostly in Virginia, which specialises in cigarette tobaccos, and Kentucky where pipe tobaccos are grown. In these areas the long humid growing season is excellent for this leafy plant, and it is an economic crop for the small farmers found there.

Most European countries grow some tobacco, the most important of them being the USSR, Bulgaria, Greece and Italy. Much is also grown in India and China, and special varieties come from Turkey and Cuba. The latter country is renowned for the making of fine cigars. Until quite recently the production of commercial tobacco in Great Britain was subject to many restrictions, with a view to securing the revenue from imports. These have now been removed, but this has made little difference to the very small quantities produced.

In recent years tobacco has been tried out in Africa, and has become established in Malawi, Zambia and Rhodesia, where the warm summers and good drainage provide suitable physical conditions. A larger proportion of this crop is exported than in any other producing country, the main market being Western Europe, particularly Britain.

A stimulant of a very different sort is OPIUM, which like tobacco has other uses, particularly medicinal. It is obtained from a species of poppy, cultivated widely in Asia and the Middle East. Most of it is used as a drug in these areas, and both production and trade are now tightly restricted by international agreement.

Animal

Apart from the major products, most parts of an animal can be profitably used. Bones are of use in making various utensils, and are also ground down to be used in the making of glue, paper, pottery and fertiliser. Cowhide is the raw material for leather, and sheepskins for the making of many items of clothing, as well as parchment. The main suppliers of these things are, broadly speaking, the same as those of other animal products, notably Australia, New Zealand, South Africa and Argentina. The temperate countries of the Northern Hemisphere are also large producers, and their consumption, as one would expect, is also large.

STUDENT WORK

1. Why does the temperate belt have a greater amount of land under cultivation than do the hot and cold regions?

2. With the aid of a sketch map, explain the natural conditions which favour the rearing of sheep in the wool-producing regions of either South Africa or South America. (Study Fig. 4 and apply the same principles to the region you choose.)

3. Study the following list of the six largest wool-producing countries in Western Europe:

	Production (in 1,000 tons)
UNITED KINGDOM	59
SPAIN	40
FRANCE	25
ITALY	15
PORTUGAL	11
IRELAND	11

Describe and account for the main features of wool production which are revealed by these figures. Comment on the changes revealed by the most recent figures you can find.

4. Write an essay on the main features of the production of raw cotton in the United States.

5. Consider the extent to which (a) Sudan and (b) south-east China have conditions well adapted to the growing of cotton.

6. Describe and account for the changes which have taken place in the importing of raw cotton into the United Kingdom between 1913 and 1970.

7. What factors have been responsible for the great concentration of jute-growing in the lower Ganges region?

8. Write an account of the production of natural fibres in either India or the USSR relating the distribution closely to the natural background.

9. What are the factors which have favoured the great concentration of rubber production in South-East Asia?

10. What are the causes of the rapid rise in the rubber production of certain African countries in recent years?

11. Write an account of vegetable oil production in West Africa, explaining the factors which influence its location. (See Fig. 10, and use your atlas to obtain information on the physical and human conditions of the area.)

12. Draw two divided bar graphs to show the world production of soya beans and the proportions coming from the main countries in 1953, 1963 and 1967. Use the figures given below:

	Million tons		
	1953	1963	1967
BRAZIL	0·1	0·3	0·7
CANADA	0·1	0·2	0·2
CHINA	9·9	10·2	10·9 (1966)
INDONESIA	0·3	0·4	0·4
JAPAN	0·4	0·3	0·2
KOREA (N. AND S.)	0·3	0·5	0·4
USSR	0·2	0·3	0·6
USA	7·3	18·2	26·5
WORLD TOTAL	18·7	30·7	41·0

Comment on the distribution of world production, and on the changes which have taken place between 1953 and 1967.

13. Write an essay on the world production of those natural fibres used mainly for making rope and cord.

Chapter 4
Metals and Other Materials

METALS, more than any other group of related products, have been responsible for the creation of the complex material civilisation which we now take so much for granted. Among these, iron takes pride of place both in the quantities which are being continuously used and in the variety of its uses.

IRON ORE

For thousands of years iron has been the most important of all metals. Once the initial difficulties of smelting had been overcome, it outstripped such rivals as copper and tin which in the form of bronze were the first metals used by man. It did this both because of its hardness and workability, and also because it is the most common metal found in nature. After the invention of coke smelting in the Industrial Revolution of the eighteenth century output soared, and today such a vast range of equipment is made of iron and steel that our own times have, with some justice, been labelled the 'Second Iron Age'.

Iron is not found in its metallic form in nature but has to be extracted by heating from iron-bearing rocks known as ores. It is present in small quantities in most rocks, often giving them a reddish appearance. For economic exploitation the necessary minimum is generally regarded as being about 20 per cent iron, and this limits it to a small number of rocks, the main ones being as follows:

COAL MEASURE ORES. These are the black and clay band ores found in the carboniferous strata around the coalfields. Their iron content is invariably above 30 per cent, but they are found only in small quantities. Because of their favourable location they were first to be used in Western Europe for coke smelting, but by the middle of the nineteenth century the more accessible ores had been worked out.

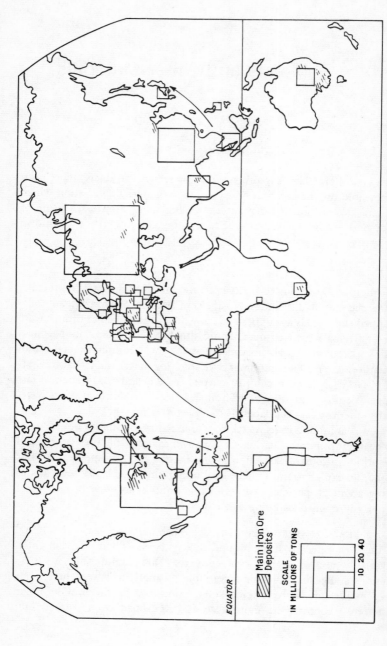

EQUATOR

Main Iron Ore
Deposits

SCALE
IN MILLIONS OF TONS

1 10 20 40

Fig. 11. World Production of Iron Ore (Iron Content Only) by Country. Arrows show Main Lines of International Trade

Since then their importance has steadily decreased, and they are now of significance only in limited areas.

JURASSIC ORES. These consist of hydrated iron laid down in the clays and limestone of the Jurassic geological era. They are the youngest rocks in which appreciable quantities of iron occur. In Great Britain there are large deposits around the north-western edge of the Central Scarplands, especially in Northampton and Lincolnshire. In eastern France, the Lorraine ore deposits are of similar type, and contain the largest known reserves of Jurassic iron. Large quantities are also found around Krivoi Rog in the Soviet Union, and the Southern Appalachians of the United States. Other countries mining this ore include West Germany, Yugoslavia and India.

It is only in relatively recent times that these ores have been exploited in a big way. The term 'minette' used for the French ores is a derogatory one as they were for long considered of little value. The main reasons for this lack of interest were:

1. They are generally located well away from the coalfields where the main centres of heavy industry grew up.

2. They contain considerable quantities of such impurities as phosphorus which could not be removed until the invention of the Gilchrist–Thomas steel furnace in the later nineteenth century. The presence of phosphorus makes iron brittle, and renders it useless for steel (see Chapter 6).

3. The iron content is low, being rarely above 30 per cent and generally a good deal lower, the English ores averaging 27·3 per cent. This has made it uneconomic to transport them long distances.

With the invention of new and more efficient steelmaking processes, and the movement of heavy industry away from the coalfields, these ores have increased in importance throughout the twentieth century. In both Britain and France they now account for over 95 per cent of all home production (Fig. 12). Much of the ore can be obtained by merely removing the topsoil, but as the more accessible deposits become exhausted mining for the deeper ones may become necessary.

HAEMATITE. This is an oxide of iron found mostly in the ancient rocks of the great 'Shields', the cores around which the continents have formed. It is also often present in the older folded strata. Great reserves exist in many parts of the world, notably around the Canadian

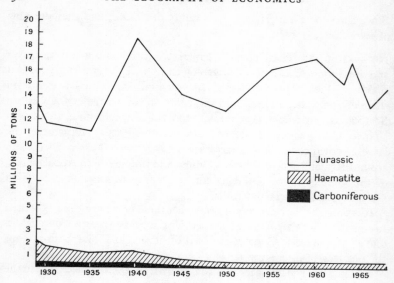

Fig. 12. Total Production of Iron Ore in Great Britain between 1929 and 1968

Shield, northern Sweden, Manchuria, India, Australia, Brazil, and northern and southern Africa. The most intensively exploited of these areas are in North America and Sweden. For the last hundred years the bulk of the North American supplies have come from the deposits west of Lake Superior. Here the ore is obtained by mining and quarrying from the folds of the 'iron ranges'. The largest supplies have come from the Mesabi range where the iron content averages 52 per cent. The Labrador ores are now of increasing importance. They were almost unknown until the end of the Second World War, but they are now believed to contain the North American continent's largest reserves. The only part of Britain having this type of ore is the Furness district of Lancashire, but exploitation here has been handicapped by the hardness of the rock and the high degree of faulting.

MAGNETITE. This magnetic ore is mostly igneous in origin, and it has an even higher iron content than that of haematite, often over 70 per cent. It is found in large quantities around Magnetogorsk in the southern Urals, and also in northern Sweden in conjunction with the haematite. The main centres of Swedish production are at Kiruna and Gallivare where most of the ore is from surface cuts (Plate 1).

World Production and Trade

The greatest producers are the USSR and some of the countries of North America and Western Europe. Apart from Canada, Sweden and Spain, they are all very large consumers, and these three countries are using increasing quantities. The movement of their ore is therefore over quite short distances, mainly going to nearby countries. The most significant international trade is that of Swedish ore to Great Britain and Germany, and Canadian ore to the United States. France and Spain are also large exporters.

In the early 1960s these countries produced three-quarters of the world's output, but by 1967 their combined total of 193 million tons was down to 57 per cent of the total. This can be explained by the steep rise in the output of certain countries, notably Australia, Brazil and those of West Africa, particularly Liberia and Mauritania. These latter produced over 17 million tons in 1967, a fourfold increase since 1963. The newer producing countries export a large proportion of their output. South America and West Africa supply the United States and Western Europe, whilst large quantities of ore from Australia and South-east Asia go to Japan. These countries have some of the largest reserves in the world, and most of them are still untapped. Brazil alone accounts for nearly a third of the world's proven reserves, and most of it is very high grade.

TABLE 3. *Output of iron ore in African countries 1960 and 1967*

	1960	1967
ANGOLA	0·4	0·7
GUINEA	0·4	0·8 (1966)
LIBERIA	2·2	12·6
MAURITANIA	—	4·8
MOROCCO	0·9	0·7
RHODESIA	0·1	0·5
SIERRA LEONE	0·9	1·3
SOUTH AFRICA	2·0	4·9
SWAZILAND	—	1·1
U.A.R.	0·1	0·2
TOTAL	7·0	27·6

The degree of exploitation of iron ore deposits has thus depended upon the following factors:

1. The nearness of the ores to areas of heavy industry.

2. Technical factors involved in exploitation. Very hard or highly faulted ores present considerable difficulties in working.

3. The problems of smelting caused by the presence of large quantities of impurities like phosphorus and sulphur.

4. The availability of other ores. If existing supplies are cheap and plentiful, there will be little reason for starting fresh ones. When supplies begin to run short it becomes necessary to look farther afield. The classic example of this was the British iron industry towards the end of the nineteenth century when it began to become increasingly dependent on foreign ores due to the gradual exhaustion of the coal-measure deposits.

In recent years the lack of adequate supplies in the industrialised countries has intensified the search for high grade ore, and the building of bulk ore carriers has made long-distance sea transport more economic.

NON-FERROUS METALS

The fact that all other metals are grouped together as 'non-irons' shows the overriding importance of the latter. Nevertheless, other metals are of considerable significance in industry, and in many ways they are usurping the functions of iron and steel. The principal among the industrial metals are copper, tin, aluminium, nickel, manganese, zinc and lead, but there are many others which have highly specialised uses. Non-ferrous metals are used in four main ways, each of which requires the use of a particular metal or metallic combination.

1. Metals used alone because their special qualities make them suitable for particular purposes. Aluminium is very light, resistant to corrosion and a good conductor of electricity. It is of especial value for the bodywork of aircraft and motor vehicles, and for domestic equipment. Also in this category come copper and lead (used for piping and exterior work as they do not corrode easily) and zinc, which is used for roofing because it is resistant, light and flexible.

2. Metals used in conjunction with another metal, generally iron, because of a special quality. Steel is often 'plated' with silver to give it lustre and value, and also with tin, a metal which does not oxidise,

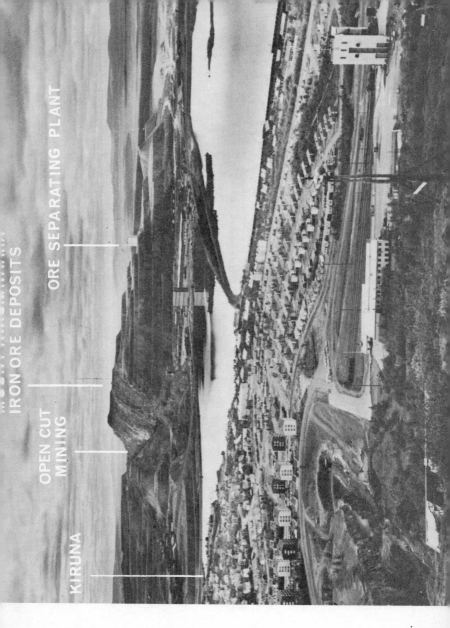

IRON ORE DEPOSITS

ORE SEPARATING PLANT

OPEN CUT MINING

KIRUNA

I. Iron ore workings at Kiruna in Northern Sweden.

ISLE OF WIGHT

THE SOLENT

II. Southampton Water, showing Britain's biggest oil refinery at Fawley (1) together with its deep water tanker terminal (2). On the eastern side of the estuary are oil storage tanks (3). Southampton docks (4) have been excavated out of a tongue of alluvium protruding between the Rivers Test and Itchen. The port is particularly well known for its transatlantic passenger traffic, and is also of considerable importance for freight. The valley of the River Itchen (5) is a natural routeway for the rail and road connections with London. The route used by ocean vessels is shown by the broken lines which enclose water with a depth of over 5 fathoms.

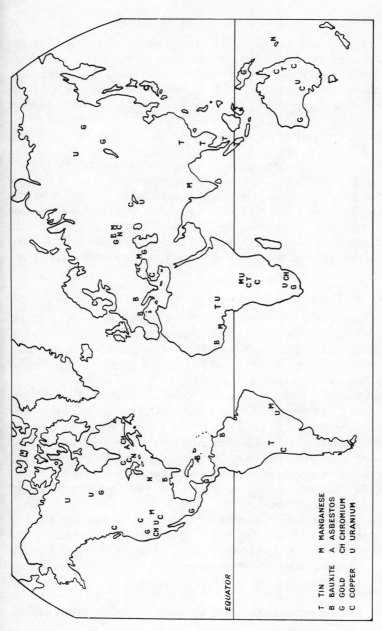

Fig. 13. The Location of Major Known Reserves of Non-Ferrous Metals

EQUATOR

T TIN   M MANGANESE
B BAUXITE   A ASBESTOS
G GOLD   CH CHROMIUM
C COPPER   U URANIUM

for food canning. The use of block tin for such purposes would be far too expensive and the desired result can easily be achieved by plating.

3. Mixing of metals to produce alloys, which have their own special qualities. Bronze was one of the earliest of these alloys made from the mixing of copper and tin. Today many metals are added to steel so as to give it particular qualities of durability, toughness and flexibility. The most important are nickel, chromium, tungsten, vanadium and molybdenum (p. 86).

4. Metals having great inherent value, such as silver and gold. They have special qualities of malleability and durability and it was these in addition to their lustre which originally made them so much sought after. They still retain their value although similar qualities can now be produced from various alloys. Added to these in recent times are radium, uranium and other radioactive materials required for nuclear fission. Production is in small quantities, and the metals are of great value.

Geological

Non-ferrous ores are, like the ores of iron, found extensively over the earth's surface (Fig. 13). They are, however, mined far more widely than is iron, and there is a considerable world trade. The ores are found in economic quantities almost entirely in very old rocks, in particular the Shields, which are made up of the oldest rocks known, and which form the cores of all the continents. Known to be particularly rich are the Canadian Shield, the African Plateau and the Australian Tableland, but all the others also contain minerals, and new reserves frequently come to light. The old fold mountains also have considerable wealth, notably the Ural mountains and the Brazilian Plateau. The old mountains of western Britain, such as the south-west peninsula, Wales and the Pennines, contain a variety of mineral ores but they are mostly found in small quantities.

Many of these metal ores occur in conjunction with one another, so areas rich in one are likely to have quantities of others too. We will now consider the production of certain metallic ores, taking an example of one used for each of the major purposes.

Aluminium

This metal is increasingly taking the place of steel in many modern industries, and is also replacing some of the other non-ferrous metals. This fact can be seen clearly from the accompanying graph (Fig. 14), which shows that world production increased over threefold between

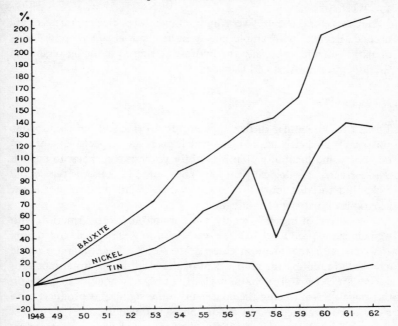

Fig. 14. Annual Percentage Change in the World Production of Bauxite, Nickel and Tin – 1948 to 1962 (1948–53 is given as a single percentage)

1948 and 1962, this being in actual terms an increase from 8 million to 25 million tons. By 1967 output was up further to over 46 million tons. Bauxite, now the principal ore, is soft and easily mined, and is different from most of the non-ferrous metals in being found in young rocks. The major producers are Jamaica, USSR, Guyana, Australia, Surinam (Dutch Guiana), the United States and France. These together account for about 70 per cent of world production. The greatest regional concentration of production can be seen to be in the New World, with the Caribbean states and the USA between them producing 60 per cent of the world total. The greatest increase in output in recent years has been that of Australia which was an insignificant producer in the early 1960s.

The USA, USSR and France are the only large producers which are also large consumers, other main consumers being Canada and Western Europe. These latter import bauxite primarily from Central America and West Africa.

Since smelting requires very high temperatures electric furnaces are needed. Regions with ample cheap electric power are therefore particularly suitable, especially the hydro-electricity producing regions of Scandinavia, the Alps and Canada.

Nickel and Tin

These two are similar in that they are used principally in conjunction with steel. Nickel is an additive which gives steel special qualities of toughness and flexibility. Tin is used for plating steel sheets to make it non-corrosive. Geologically they are both found in the same type of old rocks, but the distribution of reserves is very different, as also is the geographical pattern of production.

The output of nickel is highly concentrated in North America, with Canada alone producing half the world's supply. The great consuming areas are also the main producers, the USA, USSR and Canada together accounting for 90 per cent of the total. Other important producers are New Caledonia and Cuba. Europe is notably deficient in this metal, Poland being the continent's only significant producer, and it has to be imported from Canada and New Caledonia.

South-East Asia is the most important source of tin, the greater part of it coming from Malaysia, Indonesia, Thailand and China. These four countries are responsible for 70 per cent of world production, with Malaysia alone accounting for over 40 per cent of this. The other most important sources are Central and West Africa and Bolivia. As in so many other commodities, the Australian tin production has also increased considerably in recent years. Although only small quantities are required – world production of tin concentrate for 1967 was 174,500 tons – this is a vital and high value commodity, and so is able to stand transport over large distances to the consuming centres. This is very important since there are few metals in which the great industrial countries are so deficient (Fig. 15). The production in North America and Western Europe is insignificant, and that of the Soviet Union is undoubtedly small, although the exact amount is not known.

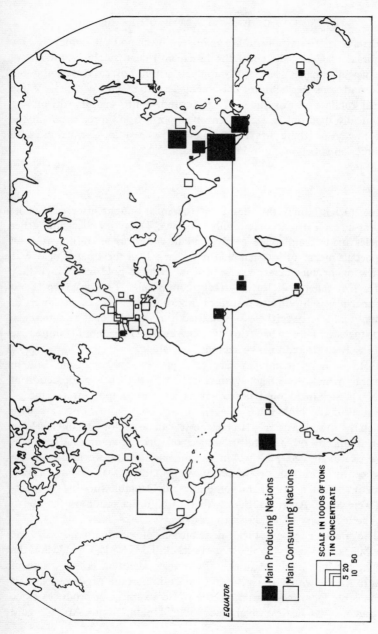

Fig. 15. World Production and Consumption of Tin Concentrate

Britain is Western Europe's main producer and all mining is now confined to Cornwall. Until the nineteenth century this country was the world's major source of supply. Output now averages about a thousand tons per annum, this being less than one per cent of the world total. Towards the end of the nineteenth century tin-mining practically died out in face of cheap imports from abroad, but in the last few years there has been renewed interest in Cornish tin and production is beginning to increase again.

Gold

Since ancient times this has been the most sought after of metals, and as a result has become highly precious. Today jewellery and other articles made from it are costly, and in the form of bullion it is an important means of international payment. Until the First World War all the major currencies were valued in terms of gold into which they were – in theory, at least – freely convertible. This was the 'Gold Standard' which fell into disuse during the depression of the interwar years. Gold is nevertheless still used for international transactions, and stocks are kept to back up paper currencies. The amounts mined are purposely restricted so as to keep up the value.

Gold is found mainly in very old rocks of igneous origin, and in minerals which have been washed out of such rocks by the action of rivers. The Shields and nearby areas are thus important producers. Because of the high value of even small deposits, and the ease with which the waterborne or 'placer' deposits can be exploited, gold has been more than any other metal the object of speculative mining, and this gave rise to the 'gold rushes' in various parts of the world during the past century. Prospectors went anywhere if there was news of a find, sometimes striking lucky and sometimes not. Notable sites for prospecting were South Australia, South Africa, California and, most famous of all, the legendary Klondike of the Yukon.

The present geographical distribution of production, with one notable exception, resembles that of nickel; the USSR, Canada and the USA, produce large quantities. The great exception is the Union of South Africa which is by far the most important producer, and is responsible for three-quarters of the world's supply. It produces twice as much as its nearest rival, the Soviet Union. South Africa's gold production comes mostly from the Witwatersrand region of the Transvaal. Here, in an area of about thirty miles by ten, the rich gold-bearing conglomerates are exploited, and the gold is exported all over the world. This great producing area is the most successful of the 'gold rush' areas and the only one where gold is found in such quantities as to have given the mining operations a degree of permanence.

OTHER MINERALS

Many of the rocks which do not yield metals are none the less of use to man. Some of these can be used in their original form, while others are of value for the substances which can be extracted from them.

Stone

This has always been one of the most important of all building materials in those areas where stone of suitable quality is to be found. Before long-distance transport or the making of substitutes became economic propositions, most building was done with local stone if any was available. Few of these stones are any longer of importance in the more technically advanced countries, unless they possess special qualities of appearance and workability. Stones which do have these include granite, marble and limestone, and these are used considerably for special building purposes. Granite is found in very old rocks, and the highlands of Britain are rich in it. Marble and limestone are found most frequently in younger strata, much marble coming from Italy and the United States. When it is broken up into chippings, stone is of use for road-building and as an ingredient of concrete (see p. 105).

A stone with very special qualities is *slate* which is very hard and has a fine and consistent cleavage. This has made it of great value as a roofing material. It is found in very old rocks, and the world's largest exploited deposits are those of North Wales. These have supplied the greater part of the needs of Britain, and large quantities have been exported to all parts of the world. During the last quarter of a century the use of other roofing materials, notably tiles, has drastically reduced the need for slates, and they are now produced on only a small scale. Much slate is now being powdered and used in the making of cement, bricks and pottery. (See Chapter 6.)

Clay

This is the raw material for a large number of things ranging from pottery to bricks. The best quality pottery is made from china clay or kaolin. This material results from the disintegration of granite, and the largest producers of it are the United States and Great Britain. Czechoslovakia, France and China also produce large quantities. In Great Britain all the supplies come from Cornwall, and much is exported as well as being sent to supply the flourishing industry of the Potteries (Stoke-on-Trent).

Chemicals

The raw materials for the chemical industry are obtained from a great variety of rocks. *Sulphur* is used in the making of sulphuric acid, insecticides and for vulcanising rubber. It is obtained both in its natural state and from pyrites. The most important producers are the United States, Mexico, Italy and France. *Nitrates* are used in fertilisers, and the world's largest deposits are in northern Chile. *Phosphates* are used in a similar way, and these come from the United States, the Soviet Union, North Africa and parts of the Pacific. *Potash* is of use in many chemical processes, and can be obtained either in the form of salts or from organic matter. Germany and France are both large producers. *Common salt* (sodium chloride) is widely distributed throughout the world, and can also be obtained from the evaporation of sea-water. Great Britain has large reserves, the biggest being those of Cheshire (see p. 119).

Mica and Asbestos

These are two minerals which have highly specialised uses. Mica breaks into pliable transparent flakes which are both heat and fire resistant. It is used for covering apertures in conditions where these qualities are essential. The greater part of the world's supplies are from India. Asbestos is also fire-proof, but unlike mica it is fibrous and may be woven. Its special use is for resistant clothing and textile materials. Over half of the world's supplies are from Canada.

STUDENT WORK

1. Discuss the relative importance of home and imported iron ore supplies in the United Kingdom. (Study Figs. 12 and 27.)

2. Write an essay on the production and uses of any two alloy metals used in steel.

3. On a map of the world, draw proportional squares to show the iron ore reserves of the ten principal countries. Use the figures given below:

	Proven reserves in million tons (countries with over 1,000 million)
BRAZIL	17,505
FRANCE	6,560
INDIA AND PAKISTAN	5,285
UNITED STATES	5,200
GREAT BRITAIN	3,760
USSR	3,140
CANADA	2,944
SWEDEN	2,400
CHINA	2,160
GERMANY (W AND E)	1,510

Compare this with Fig. 11 (Iron ore production) and attempt an explanation of the differences between the distributions shown.

4. Suggest reasons for the renewed interest now being shown in Cornish tin.

5. Describe the distribution of ferrous and non-ferrous metal reserves on the African continent, pointing out the main areas of production.

6. Study carefully the maps for the production and consumption of rubber (Fig. 8) and tin (Fig. 15). Comment on the differences you note between the distribution of production and consumption in each case.

7. Write an account of the iron ore supplies (home and imported) of the United States.

8. Write an account of the production of non-metallic minerals in the United Kingdom, relating this to the geological background.

Chapter 5

Power Supplies

POWER is energy, and it can be produced in many different ways. Man has harnessed a large number of nature's latent power supplies, in order to provide himself with heat, light and motive power. These come from a variety of sources:

ANIMAL. This is the oldest means used by man to supplement his own energy, horses and oxen being two of the most important animals. Although they are of diminishing importance, they are still used widely as beasts of burden in many parts of the world.

MECHANICAL. The older and more primitive forms of this are the use of wind for sailing boats, and both wind and water to drive mills and work pumps. These things are still very common in underdeveloped countries, although far less so in the industrial ones. During the present century water power has returned to the scene in more potent form than ever as a means of generating electric power.

CHEMICAL. This is power produced by the combustion of carbon either from living matter like wood, or from fossilised organic materials such as coal, peat, petroleum and natural gas. It is this group which has dominated power production in the industrial countries.

NUCLEAR. This is the generation of energy through the fission of highly radioactive materials such as uranium and plutonium. It has only been accomplished during the last twenty years, and its economic significance is as yet small.

The particular methods of power generation which are of overriding economic significance are coal, petroleum, natural gas and hydro-electricity.

COAL

Coal has been for over 150 years the most important single source of industrial power. It is composed of the fossilised remains of a dense forest vegetation which covered large parts of the earth's surface millions of years ago. Most reserves date from the carboniferous geological period (250–300 million years ago), but coal and similar substances are found in both younger and older rocks than these. Subsequent earth movements have buckled up the originally horizontal strata, and the degree to which this has taken place has determined the present angle and depth of the deposits. In some places, such as parts of North-East England, the coal can literally be gathered off the surface, while in other places, like the concealed northern extension of the Ruhr coalfield in Germany, it is thousands of feet deep. Different coals also vary considerably in their qualities, and consequently in the purposes for which they are likely to be suitable.

BITUMINOUS COAL. This is easily worked and burns quickly with a hot flame. Economically it is the most important of all coals, and its combustibility, brought about by a high proportion of volatile matter, multiplies its uses. Coking coals are those which convert readily into coke for use in blast furnaces, and gas coals reduce easily in retorts. Steam coals are well adapted for powering engines, while domestic coals give off heat for longer periods. It is because of this great flexibility that bituminous coal has always been in demand, and although certain of its uses are diminishing, newer ones, such as the generating of electricity, are replacing them.

ANTHRACITE. This is a very pure form of coal with a high carbon content. It is hard and burns slowly, and this makes it of little use for many industrial purposes. With the invention of the slow-burning stove at the end of the last century, production increased considerably, and it is still mined in large quantities in certain areas.

LIGNITE. Although not really coal at all in the strictest sense, this is sometimes referred to as 'brown coal'. It is geologically more recent than the others, and so its distribution is different. Its low carbon content limits its usefulness considerably, but in the countries where it

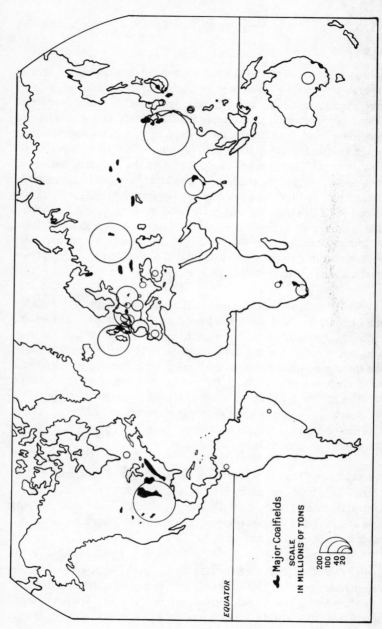

SCALE
IN MILLIONS OF TONS

Major Coalfields

200
100
40
20

EQUATOR

Fig. 16. World Coal Production by Country

is mined it is of considerable importance domestically and for conversion into electric power.

World Coal Production

The earliest mining took place where the coal was most readily got at, for example, on outcrops and seams approaching near to the surface. Subsequent mining operations in the industrial countries have moved to greater and greater depths. This became necessary because of the exhaustion of the older workings and because, as the demand grew, the necessary supplies could only be found deeper down. Steadily improving techniques of mining made this greater depth possible.

World coal production (excluding lignite) is now running at about 2,000 million tons per annum. This comes from about fifty countries, but the greater part of it from a dozen only. China, the USSR, the USA, Great Britain, West Germany and Poland are the most important, accounting for over 100 million tons each. India, Japan, France and South Africa are also high on the list of producers. It will be seen from Fig. 16 that the great centres of production are overwhelmingly concentrated in the Northern Hemisphere. Geologically the coalfields are situated on an east–west axis stretching through Europe and Asia along the northern edge of the mountains of Hercynian and Alpine age. In North America 90 per cent of the coal comes from the Appalachian mountains, and their northern extension into Canada's maritime provinces. These mountains are of similar age to their European and Asian counterparts.

Production in Great Britain

While world production of coal has increased throughout the present century, the production graphs for different countries reveal considerable variations. Great Britain was the first country to use coal on a large scale for industrial purposes, and remained the world's largest producer until the end of the nineteenth century when she was overtaken by the United States (Fig. 18). Great Britain had the advantage of large and accessible reserves, together with a wide range of high-quality coals. Her production continued to rise until 1913 when it reached the record total of 292 million tons. This was a time when coal was indisputably the most important industrial fuel, and the general efficiency of the British industry enabled it to compete favourably all over the world with locally mined coals. After 1918 the demand began to fluctuate considerably, but in recent years production has stabilised at a much lower level than that of 1913.

The older mines were almost always found on the edges of the coalfields, but mining has spread steadily towards their centres. In some coalfields the workable deposits dip far beneath younger rocks, and during the present century they also have been exploited. In the York–Derby–Notts and Durham coalfields of northern England this has resulted in a steady eastwards movement of mining, and many of the larger mines are no longer on the exposed coalfield at all. The newer mines have invariably been much bigger than the older ones, and their numbers much smaller.

There are a large number of coalfields in Britain, but most of them are small, and output is dominated by the 'Big Five', namely York–Derby–Notts, Durham, South Wales, Lanark and Lancashire. The largest and most efficient of these is the York–Derby–Notts (Fig. 17 (1)). This,

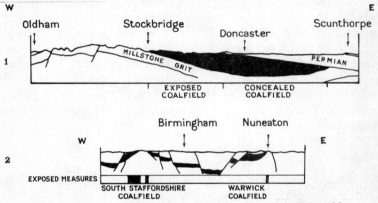

Fig. 17. Sections through British Coalfields. 1. The York–Derby–Notts. 2. The Midland Coalfields. All coal measures coloured black

together with adjacent Midland fields, has an abundance of easily mined deep coal and an excellent location for transport to the consumers (Fig. 40). The South Wales and Scottish fields have certain unfavourable geological features, but in the case of South Wales this is compensated for by the ease of transport to the nearby heavy industries. To make itself more competitive at the present day, the industry has been considerably modernised and 'rationalised'. Besides mechanisation this means fewer and larger mines and a reduction in the numbers employed in them.

Decline of the Older Producers

What has been said of the developments in the British industry is also in large measure true of coal-mining in other West European countries and in North America. Some of the important reasons for this decline in production are:

1. The competition from other fuels, particularly petroleum, natural gas and hydro-electric power. In 1913 coal accounted for 95 per cent of the world's energy consumption, while by 1962 this had been reduced to 50 per cent and by 1968 to 30 per cent. In the United States it is now only 24 per cent and in Italy 9 per cent. In the United Kingdom, where coal accounts for 93 per cent of the home energy production, coal (including derived sources, such as electricity and gas) now makes up 55 per cent of energy consumption, the deficit being made up mostly by petroleum and natural gas imports. These new fuels are being used for such things as motor transport where coal is of no use, and they are even replacing coal for powering locomotives, electricity generation and heating.

2. The decrease in world coal trade. Before the First World War, Britain was exporting 80 million tons annually, and found markets for it all over the world. By 1963 this had been reduced to 7·5 million and in 1968 was only 2·7 million. The competition of other fuels has again contributed to this, but there is also the increased production in the former importing countries themselves. This has made them more self-sufficient and so in need of fewer imports.

3. Uneconomic production. Many of the older producing regions, like Belgium and Scotland, are finding it difficult to compete economically either in price or in quantity. Many factors contribute to this situation, such as the working out of seams, geological difficulties, antiquated equipment and high labour costs. In Belgium, coal output has decreased by 20 per cent since 1948 and it is now cheaper to import coal from the neighbouring mining areas, particularly the Ruhr. The free market created by the European Coal and Steel Community (see p. 214) has brought the problem more out into the open, and it has

been necessary to subsidise uncompetitive regions to minimise hardship in them. In the United States, Pennsylvania is a similar problem area, and considerable economic disruption has been caused by over-production in relation to the decrease in demand.

The Newer Producers

Those nations which have only during the present century become large producers have shown different tendencies, and in most of them output has steadily increased since 1945. Between 1948 and 1967 the USSR's annual production increased from 150 million to 414 million tons. In the former year this was only a quarter that of the United States, while by 1961 it had become almost equal, although the USA has now drawn ahead again. The Donbas in the Ukraine accounts for about 42 per cent of the Soviet output, and other important coalfields are those of Karaganda and the Kuzbas in Siberia. Even more rapid has

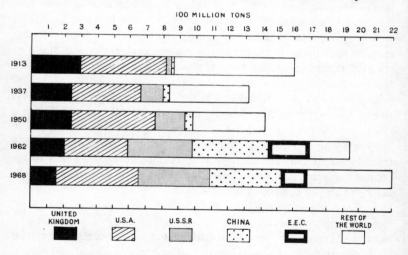

Fig. 18. The Four Largest Coal Producers. Totals for Selected Years

been China's increase in production, most of this coming from Manchuria and the north of the country. This growth has been due to the greatly increased needs of the economy, together with China's richness in easily worked coal. Its significance to China, as indeed to most of the newer industrial countries, is considerably greater than it is in the older industrial countries.

Lignite

The world production of lignite is about 720 million tons per annum. This is nearly a third of that of bituminous and anthracite combined, but its value in terms of energy is far less than this would suggest. Production is very highly concentrated into the European countries and the USSR, which among them account for 90 per cent. Apart from West Germany, with around 100 million tons, practically all this comes from the countries of east Europe, led by East Germany which alone has an output of 240 million tons. In these countries it is used in place of coal, and much of it is converted into briquettes for locomotives, generating electricity and domestic use.

PETROLEUM

Petroleum is, in all senses, a newer fuel than coal. Geologically it is found in more recent rocks, and economically it is more adapted to modern fuel needs. Large-scale exploitation is essentially a thing of the present century, and between 1913 and 1968 world output increased thirty times from 54 million to 2,000 million tons. Over this same period that of coal rose less than three times from 696 million to 1,800 million tons, and in recent years it has been falling. This late, but rapid development as compared to coal can be attributed to a number of factors:

   1. The largest reserves are found far from the established industrial regions, often in areas which are sparsely populated and primitive.
   2. While coal can be used in its original form, petroleum has first to be refined to make it into useful fuel. This is a complicated process which requires a considerable degree of technical skill.
   3. The uses of petroleum are more specialised than those of coal. Overwhelmingly the most important is that of powering the internal combustion engine, which has come into large-scale use only during the present century. Even today this fuel has not generally become an important localising factor in industry.
   Petroleum is petrified carbon in liquid form, and it results from

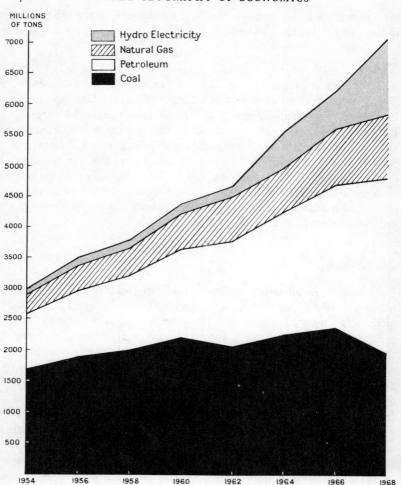

Fig. 19. World Energy Output by Source 1954–68. Figures in millions of metric tons coal equivalent

animal and vegetable matter being sealed in the rocks. It then moves along permeable strata until it is brought to a stop by an 'oil trap'. These traps can be created by faults and intrusions which break off the strata, or by anticlines which prevent the further movement of the liquid (Fig. 20). The most likely areas for finding petroleum are gently folded depressions in young rock formations and near to recent mountain chains. The largest reserves appear to be found in quite

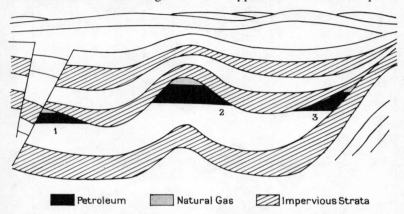

Petroleum   Natural Gas   Impervious Strata

Fig. 20. Oil Traps. 1. A fault. 2. An anticline. 3. A stratigraphic trap

small areas, and the most important in order of present production are as follows:

North America

All three of the large North American countries produce petroleum, and the continent as a whole now accounts for about a third of the world total. The United States, accounting for over 90 per cent of the continent's output, is the most important producer in the world. Her major oilfields are in Texas and on the Great Plains to the north of it, and there is also considerable production in California. The United States was first in the field as a petroleum producer, and the immense increase in output after 1918 led to fears that the reserves would soon become exhausted. As a result, a quota system was introduced, and any excess of demand over this has now to be made up by imports. Canada was not a producer until 1945, but since then it has been discovered that considerable quantities lie beneath parts of the Prairie provinces, especially Alberta. This area has now become an important producer, and makes a substantial contribution to the country's energy requirements.

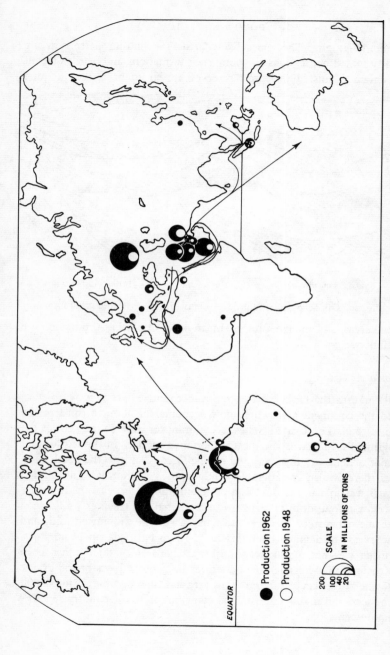

EQUATOR

● Production 1962
○ Production 1948

SCALE
IN MILLIONS OF TONS

200
100
40
20

Fig. 21. World Petroleum Production by Country, 1948 and 1962. Arrows show principal lines of trade

The Middle East

The output of this area represents about one-quarter of the world's total and is centred around Mesopotamia and the Persian Gulf. It is shared among a large number of states ranging in size from Iran (1,648,000 sq. km or 650,000 square miles) to Bahrain (600 sq. km or 213 square miles). Some of the smaller Gulf States have huge oil potentials, and in 1968 Kuwait produced 122 million tons. Other important producers are Saudi-Arabia and Iraq (Fig. 22). Middle

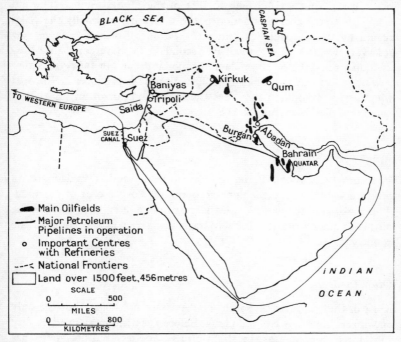

Fig. 22. Petroleum Production in the Middle East

Eastern oil only became of importance after the First World War, but a large part of the national incomes of these states is now made up of royalties from its sale. An outlier of the Middle Eastern oil province extends through Egypt into North Africa, and this is now being considerably developed. Algeria, which only started producing oil in 1958, had an output of 42 million tons in 1968. Even more spectacular has been the rise of Libyan production which did not commence until well after Algeria but had reached 126 million tons by 1968. This made her the second Arab producer – after Saudi-Arabia – and sixth in the whole world.

The USSR and Eastern Europe

The rapid growth of the oil industry in the Soviet Union has now made her output second only to that of the United States. The old established centre of production is the Caucasus, especially the Baku region by the Caspian Sea. Since the Second World War large new reserves, which have been called 'Second Baku' have come into production around the southern flanks of the Urals, and in 1964 there were new finds farther east. The largest East European producer is Romania which, with 13 million tons, has the largest output of any European country if one discounts the USSR.

South America

Venezuela, Colombia, Peru, Argentina, Brazil and Trinidad are all producers, but Venezuela alone accounts for 80 per cent of the total. This makes her the world's third largest source of supply. Most of the oil here comes from the Lake Maracaibo district in the north of the country.

Other Producers

Most of the countries of South-East Asia are producers, but the only one of real importance is Indonesia. Before 1945 Indonesia made a very substantial contribution to the world's supplies, but its share has decreased as the production of other countries has increased. Apart from Romania, the most important European producer is West Germany, in which production increased thirteen times between 1948 and 1968. Even so its 8 million tons per annum is but a fraction of its needs. France, the Netherlands and Austria also produce appreciable quantities, and Britain's very small output comes mainly from Nottinghamshire.

World Trade

Petroleum is one of the most important commodities entering into world trade at the present day. This is because (1) it has become a vital part of the energy supplies of the advanced nations, and is also used considerably in the chemicals and synthetics industries. However, particularly in the European countries and Japan, the demand is far greater than the very limited home supplies. (2) Many of the great world producers have a considerable excess of supply over demand, and therefore petroleum is of most use to them as an export.

The greatest single slice of the international trade is between the West European countries with their huge demand, and those of the Mediterranean and the Middle East with the largest known reserves in the world. Of Britain's total imports of crude oil (83 million tons in 1968) 65 per cent originated in the Middle East, and 30 per cent in Kuwait alone. Refined products make up only a quarter of Britain's imports, and the greater part of these are from Latin America and Western Europe. The countries of Western Europe now also receive large supplies of petroleum from Algeria and the USSR, the latter also sending oil to the countries of Eastern Europe.

As well as being the world's largest producer, the United States is also a large importer in order to satisfy the immense home demand. Most of her supplies come from Venezuela and other Latin American countries. About a third of these are refined or partially refined products, which make up 37 per cent of Venezuela's oil exports. In the Middle East the proportion of refined products is now far smaller, being about 13 per cent in the case of Iran. In most of the producing areas local consumption is now increasing as a result of industrial and other developments, and the proportion exported is therefore diminishing.

Oil Refining

Before it can be used as a fuel, petroleum has first to be separated or fractionated into its constituent parts, which are then used for a variety of different purposes. This process is known as refining, and it has to be carried out at large and complex establishments. The most important of their products are petrol, fuel oil, kerosene, gas oil, diesel oil, lubricants and many chemical derivatives.

Refineries are built in two types of location. They can be on or near to the oilfields, so that the petroleum products are transported in their refined form to the markets. Alternatively, they can be near to the markets, in which case it is the crude petroleum which has to be transported the longest distances. Before the Second World War oilfield locations were most in favour, and a large proportion of the oil was transported refined or partly refined. In the Persian Gulf the great Abadan oil refinery, for example, handled a great deal of the oil destined for Europe. In the last twenty years the trend has been towards more refining in the consuming countries, and this has resulted in the building of large numbers of refineries in Western Europe. The most important refining centres in this region are Rotterdam, the Ruhr, the lower Seine, Marseilles, Hamburg, Milan and Genoa. In recent years new refineries have been established around the coasts of Italy, notably at Naples, Milazzo and Priolo, the two latter in Sicily. In the United States, although there is considerable refining at the oilfields, some of the largest refineries are in the north-east, particularly at New York, Philadelphia, Baltimore, Toledo and Chicago.

Refining in Great Britain

The refinery output of Great Britain increased from 2·4 million tons in 1938 to 90 million tons in 1969. In the former year 80 per cent of the country's oil imports were of refined products, while in 1969 this proportion had dropped to about 20 per cent. Although there are seventeen refineries in use, 75 per cent of the output comes from the five largest, these being Fawley, Kent, Stanlow, Shell Haven and Llandarcy. Each of these has a capacity of over 5 million tons per annum. It will be seen (Table 4) that practically all the refineries are either coastal or estuarine, and that the largest number of them are found in the south of the country. The main factors influencing their locations are as follows:

1. The presence of a deep-water terminal able to take the large vessels in which the oil is imported. This has become ever more necessary as the size of the tankers has increased and the number of ports able to take them has consequently diminished. Fawley, the largest of the refineries, has an excellent deep-water site near Southampton (Plate II), and Milford Haven, first used for oil importing in 1960, is situated on a natural harbour without rival, which will take the largest of modern

tankers. Many of the best importing points now send petroleum by pipeline to other refineries or to users. It is pumped from Milford

TABLE 4. *The capacity of British refineries*

REFINERY	CAPACITY (in million tons)	
	1964	1970
FAWLEY	11·5	16·5
SHELL HAVEN	8·9	9·8
ISLE OF GRAIN	9·5	10·0
STANLOW	6·1	10·5
LLANDARCY	5·5	8·0
MILFORD HAVEN*	4·8	14·4
GRANGEMOUTH	3·3	7·0
CORYTON	2·4	7·0
HEYSHAM	2·0	2·0
BILLINGHAM	1·0	5·0
TEESPORT	—	6·0
KILLINGHOLME	—	10·5

* Three refineries

Haven to the Llandarcy refinery, and from the excellent harbour at Finnart (Loch Long) to Grangemouth.

2. The refining is best done at or near to the importing points because of the bulk nature of the raw material, and the consequent high costs of transporting it by land. Estuarine sites enable the tankers to penetrate farther and so lessen the costs considerably. Both Stanlow and Grangemouth are more centrally placed for distribution of their products than would have been purely coastal sites.

3. Proximity to the main consuming centres is a further advantage. The south of the country, with its lack of coal and its light industries, is the largest consuming area, and this has encouraged the location of refineries around its coasts. Of the total British capacity, 70 per cent is located either on or south of a line from Milford Haven to the Thames, and the Thames estuary alone accounts for 25 per cent.

4. The shorter sea journey also originally favoured sites in the south of the country, since northern ones add considerably to the distance travelled. This has not prevented the erection of refineries in the north so long as there is a demand for the products.

NATURAL GAS

In many of the world's oilfields natural gas is found in association with petroleum. Except in the USA, however, it remained almost unused until after the Second World War, and in 1948 the USA was still responsible for 95 per cent of the world's output. Today it is still far and away the leader, and its 550 million cubic metres is over 60 per cent of the world's total. The gas is transported by pipeline, and a great network of these now connects the main producing and consuming centres (p. 198). This fuel is now responsible for nearly one-third of the total energy consumption of the United States.

The other main producers are the USSR, parts of South America, Algeria and Western Europe. In this latter area, gas has been found in Germany, France, Italy and the Netherlands, the latter country having some of the largest reserves known to exist. Imports have been handicapped by the problems of transport over long distances, but the new method of liquefaction is removing this obstacle. During the 1960s large reserves of natural gas were discovered under the North Sea, and these are now contributing to the home needs of Great Britain and other adjacent countries. In 1968 natural gas was responsible for about 4 per cent of the total energy consumption of Western Europe.

HYDRO-ELECTRIC POWER

Running water has for thousands of years been used to provide power for a variety of purposes, but its use for the generation of electricity is quite new. It was in North America that this flexible, clean and rapidly transported power was first produced on a large scale, but it is now generated in every continent in the world, and gigantic power projects are revolutionising the economic potential of many an unpromising region.

The best conditions for hydro-electric power are found in areas having some at least of the following features:

1. A good annual rainfall in the water catchment areas ranging from minima of 500 to 1,000 mm (20 to 40 inches) (depending on temperatures) and coming throughout the year.

2. Impermeable rocks to ensure maximum surface drainage and to allow for water storage, whether natural or artificial.

3. Moderate temperatures in the places where the water is being stored. Very cold conditions cause the water to freeze and so interfere with its use; very high temperatures, on the other hand, cause a great deal of loss from evaporation.

4. Steep slopes to provide the necessary head of water. Narrowly incised valleys such as are found in glaciated uplands are very suitable for the building of dams.

Even this fairly rigorous list of natural conditions is not all. The installations needed – dams, pipelines, power stations, transmission lines – are more costly than those for any other type of power. Therefore ample long-term capital investment is essential, together with ready markets at hand for the power. Although today electric power can be transported long distances, this naturally makes it more expensive. The following are the main areas of production:

North America

With an output of 360,000 gigawatt hours (1 gigawatt hour = 10 million kilowatt hours), the USA and Canada together account for 36 per cent of the world's total. The main producing areas are south-east Canada, the southern Appalachians and the western Rockies. In the southern Appalachians a great part of the generating is in the hands of the Tennessee Valley Authority, which was set up in 1934 to help guide the economic development of a formerly backward area. Power from the Tennessee dams is sold over large areas, and it has been of great importance in developing local industries. The western parts of the United States generate 40 per cent of its hydro-electricity. Such dams as the Hoover, Shasta, Grand Coolee and Parker use the deep and fast western rivers to make power available over large areas which have few other sources of supply.

In Canada the dependence on this form of power is much greater, and it supplies 75 per cent of the country's electricity, as compared to 15 per cent in the USA. Around the south-east edges of the Canadian Shield the steep slopes, impermeable strata, lakes and good water supply make excellent natural conditions. There is a large market as a result of rapid industrialisation coupled with the inadequacy of other power sources. Much electricity is generated on the St Lawrence itself which is an infamously capricious river for navigation. Its disadvantages as a route-way, however, become assets for producing power, and one of the most famous installations is at Niagara Falls between Lakes Erie and Ontario (Plate III).

Western Europe

This region produces just over two-thirds as much hydro-electric power as does North America, and in most countries its development has been quite recent. This is both because of the great importance of other types of fuel, especially coal, and because many of the nations have been unable to afford the necessary capital investment. Since 1945 there has been considerable development, particularly in the mountains of Scandinavia, the Alps and the Pyrenees. The largest output comes from Sweden, Italy, Norway, France and Switzerland, and in all these countries this form of power is now making a substantial contribution to the national requirements (Fig. 23). One of its greatest advantages is that it brings modern power to mountainous and hitherto poor areas which are much in need of it. It has also done much to supplement power sources in other regions. France has long been handicapped by her poverty in good-quality coal supplies, and since 1945 she has undertaken a large programme of hydro-electric installations mainly in the Alps, the Pyrenees and the Rhône valley. Her production now totals 50,000 gigawatt hours, which represents 43 per cent of all her electricity (Fig. 23). In Great Britain hydro-electricity is responsible for only about 2 per cent of the nation's production. Most of the generating stations are in Western Scotland and North Wales.

The Soviet Union

One of Lenin's famous sayings was that 'Communism is Soviet power plus electrification', and it has always been one of the prime tasks of the Soviet government to increase its electricity output. Surprisingly the number of Soviet dams is quite small – forty-four in all – but many of them are very large and have an immense power potential. Total production in 1968 was 100 million gigawatt hours, and this makes it come third after the United States and Canada. The main rivers harnessed are those of the south and centre of European Russia, par-

III. Beauharnois hydro-electric power station on the St Lawrence River, Canada. By damming the river at this point the necessary head of water has been provided. It also ensures an even flow of water into the St Lawrence Seaway.

IV. The Fairless Works near Trenton is one of the largest integrated iron and steel plants in the United States. The iron ore is imported by sea (1) and stored at the quaysides (2). It is then fed into the blast furnaces (3) which get their fuel from the coking plant (4). In the rear are the steel and tin-plating mills (5).

ticularly the Dnieper, Don and Volga, where the natural conditions are most favourable. More recently production has been increasing in

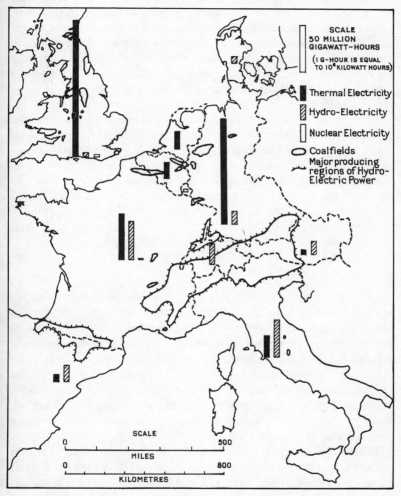

Fig. 23. The Output of Electric Power in Western Europe

Central Siberia, and the installations at Bratsk on the Angara river are the largest in the world.

Other Regions

In many other parts of the world hydro-electricity is increasingly being used to supplement deficiencies in other sources. Japan, with its mountainous terrain and heavy rainfall, is a large producer, now fourth in the world, and in India its importance is considerable especially in the north. In Australia the great Snowy Mountains scheme is one of the most ambitious ever undertaken, and is not due to be fully completed until 1975. In the African countries considerable reliance is being placed on its development; this is dealt with fully in Chapter 10.

As a source of power hydro-electricity has many advantages besides being well adapted to modern needs. It is not a diminishing or variable asset, and so can be relied on to go on producing in predictable quantities. It is also, in most places, an upland or mountain resource, which can take power to local industries such as metal refining, timber and pulp milling. There is immense potential in all continents, but one of the greatest barriers to its realisation is the need for very large capital investment.

NUCLEAR POWER

There are many other minor power sources, like peat, wood, thermal springs and wind, and all of them have their own particular applications. Nuclear energy deserves special mention, less for its present contribution, which is small, than for the possibilities it opens up for the future. The first nuclear reaction took place in Chicago in 1943, and that event initiated what has come to be loosely referred to as the 'Atomic Age'. So far most of this power has been used for making weapons of war, and progress in its peaceful uses has lagged behind. However, most of the industrial nations now have programmes of research into its peaceful uses.

Britain has been in the forefront of this development, and her first nuclear power station was completed at Calder Hall in 1952. As a result of the experience gained here, and at research establishments such as Harwell, a full-scale programme for the construction of nuclear power stations was initiated in 1955. The capacity in 1963 was 925 megawatts, representing about 4 per cent of the national electricity production for that year, while by 1968 it was 4,000 megawatts, this being 12 per cent of production. Britain's output in 1968 was nearly a half of the world's total and was three times as great as that of continental Europe. The principal raw material used is uranium, the main sources for which at present are Canada, Central Africa and parts of Western Europe. Although all British supplies have to be imported, they are needed in minute quantities compared with those of most other raw materials.

On the European continent a nuclear energy programme, 'Euratom', was set up in conjunction with the Common Market (Chapter 11). This is now engaged in considerable research, and the uranium deposits of France, mainly in the Massif Central, are the main home source of raw materials. The United States now produces about a quarter of the world total, and is steadily increasing her output.

As in the case of hydro-electricity, the cost of nuclear power stations is very high, and this is likely to confine their construction to the richer countries for some time to come. Besides this they are not as yet necessary in countries which possess large sources of power of their own, but are of great attraction to those which at present have power deficits.

STUDENT WORK

1. Write a comparative account of the main features of the coal industries of the United States and the Soviet Union.
2. What factors have contributed to making Ruhr coal more competitive in the markets of Western Europe than is Belgian coal?
3. Using the figures for 1962 given below, draw divided circles (pie graphs) to show the production of various forms of energy in France and West Germany:

	France	West Germany
	(in million tons coal equivalent)	
COAL AND LIGNITE	54	174
PETROLEUM	3	8
NATURAL GAS	5·3	1·2
HYDRO-ELECTRICITY	4·8	1·6

Using your graphs as a guide, compare and contrast the main features of production shown here with the most recent available statistics.

4. Using the information given below, analyse the main sources of Britain's petroleum supply, and attempt to explain the main reasons for this distribution.

British Petroleum Imports

	million metric tons
KUWAIT	18
IRAQ	11·2
LIBYA	8·8
VENEZUELA	6·4
IRAN	3·7
NIGERIA	3·3
BAHRAIN	3·3

5. Write an account of the distribution of oil refining in Western Europe (excluding the United Kingdom), and point out the factors which have influenced its distribution.

6. Discuss the relative merits of Tees-side, Thames-side and Swansea Bay as locations for oil refineries.

7. Consider carefully the following figures for production and trade in crude oil:

	Production	Exports	Imports
	(in million metric tons)		
USA	425·1	0·5	62·5
USSR	224·0	23·3	–
IRAQ	63·4	45·8	–
UK	0·1	–	59·5

(a) Work out the imports and exports as percentages of the total productions of each country.

(b) Describe and account for the significant features of their trade.

8. With the aid of a sketch map, explain why hydro-electric power has been so successful in Scandinavia.

9. What are the difficulties in the way of developing hydro-electric power in the great river basins of northern Siberia?

10. Why does hydro-electricity account for only 2 per cent of the United Kingdom's electricity production, while it accounts for 40 per cent of that of Italy?

11. Describe briefly the main features of the United States natural gas industry. What advantages enabled the United States to be first in developing this form of power?

12. Discuss the relative merits of pipelines and oil tankers in transporting Middle Eastern oil to Western European consuming centres. (See Chapter 11.)

Chapter 6
Basic Manufacturing Industry

MANUFACTURE is adding value to natural products by so altering them as to make them of greater use. A large range of the goods used by man now come into this category, but the degree of change and its complexity vary considerably. The extraction of juice from fruit, for instance, is manufacture, and so is the making of an automatic washing machine. It goes without saying that the latter is a far more complicated operation. The simple forms of manufacture can be carried out in most places provided they have the necessary raw materials, but more complex manufacturing is far more exacting in its choice of sites.

As a result modern large-scale manufacture has come to be concentrated into very limited parts of the world, and these all possess the same sorts of advantages for it. As with the growing of crops, different types of manufacture have their special requirements, and these are discussed in this and the following chapter. Manufacture generally takes place in two stages: the preparation of the materials and the making of the finished articles. In modern industry the first stage, 'basic' manufacture, is concerned with such things as iron and steel, cement, construction materials, heavy chemicals and metal refining. Certain of these are discussed together with their raw materials; others constitute well-defined industrial activities of great importance.

THE IRON AND STEEL INDUSTRY

Ferrous metals are responsible for over 90 per cent of all the metal used in the world. They underlie a great variety of industries, and their products are the basis of metal goods ranging in size from locomotives to cutlery and household equipment.

The Process

Until the end of the eighteenth century iron was usually obtained from its ore by smelting it in furnaces fired by charcoal. It was then that coke came into general use as a fuel, first of all in Great Britain and then in other countries. The method used was that developed by Abraham Darby at Coalbrookdale, and the iron so produced was very brittle and liable to crack under strain. These disadvantages were to a certain extent overcome by the invention of the reverberatory furnace at the end of the eighteenth century. This reduced the carbon content of the metal and so made it into wrought iron, which is stronger and more flexible.

The toughest form of iron is steel, which is made by fixing the carbon content at a low level. It was known long before the Industrial Revolution, but until the mid-nineteenth century it could be made only in small quantities and at considerable expense. In 1855 Bessemer invented his converter which lowered the carbon content by passing a current of air through the molten iron. This method, however, had the disadvantage of not removing the phosphorus, which makes steel brittle, and so could only be used with ores almost free from this substance. It was not until 1878 that this situation was remedied by Gilchrist–Thomas's invention of the open hearth furnace which used dolomite to remove the phosphorus and so was able to take most ores.

Today coke is still the principal fuel, since most coals are far too brittle to stand the strain of the 'charge' of ore. Limestone is added as a flux to help purify the metal, and the resulting product is known as pig iron. In the making of steel, the open hearth 'basic' process is now general, since besides taking low-grade ores it will also smelt scrap. Bessemer converters are still common in places having access to high quality ores. A new development of much significance is the injection of oxygen into the furnace to speed up the process.

SPECIAL STEELS. Further advances in steel technology have now made it possible to regulate the particular qualities required in the metal. In this the addition of non-ferrous alloys is very important, each one being used for a different purpose. Nickel steel, made with the addition of 3 per cent of this alloy, is very tough and flexible. Manganese steel requires 12–14 per cent manganese and is extremely hard. Chrome steel is made by adding 2 per cent chrome so giving the metal elasticity, and for stainless steel 13 per cent of this alloy is added. Other additives are vanadium, which in small quantities lightens the metal, and tungsten for high-speed steel. Of increasing importance is molybdenum which is much favoured by the chemical industry because of the non-corrosive qualities it gives to the steel.

Integrated Iron and Steel Plant

In view of the close association of all the processes in iron and steel making, it is very desirable that they should be carried out as closely together as possible. This has become even more so since the bulk of the pig iron now produced is intended for making into steel. When the pig has to be taken to a separate steelworks it must first be cooled down, and then resmelted, so causing considerable waste of heat besides the transport costs. The answer to this has been the development of the integrated plant, which is equipped to carry out all operations from unloading the iron ore to rolling the finished steel. Besides having blast furnaces and steelworks, such a site will also have its own rolling mills, and a large plant will have coke ovens and even its power station (see Plate IV).

World Steel Production

The world's output of steel is over 500 million tons, and the greater part of it comes from three economic regions. These are Western Europe, North America and the Comecon countries, and among them they account for 85 per cent of the world total (see fig. 24).

WESTERN EUROPE. This is the second largest of the three, and in combination its countries produced 140 million tons in 1968. Most important are West Germany, the United Kingdom, France and Italy, which together are responsible for 75 per cent of it. The largest continental iron and steel areas are the Ruhr, Franco-Belgian and Saar coalfields, together with Lorraine and south Luxemburg. Newer coastal sites have of late become more important, notably the North Sea coastal projects, and the Italian centres of Genoa, Piombino, Naples and Taranto. This latter has a large integrated plant opened in 1964 as part of a scheme to develop the Italian south. The main centre of the Italian industry is the north, particularly Milan.

NORTH AMERICA. This is the world's largest producer, with an output

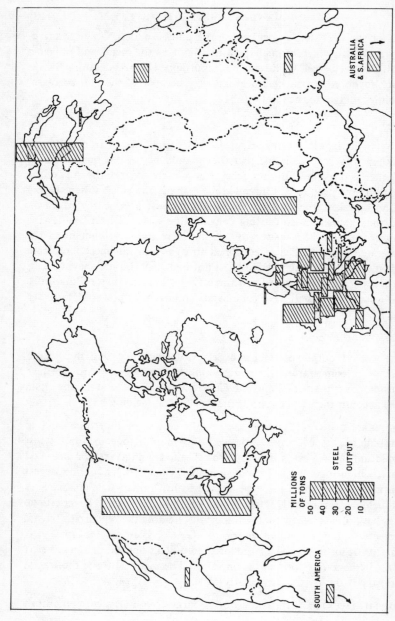

Fig. 24. World Steel Production by Country

of over 130 million tons. More than 90 per cent of it comes from the United States, which has the world's largest single output. This will be considered in more detail later on.

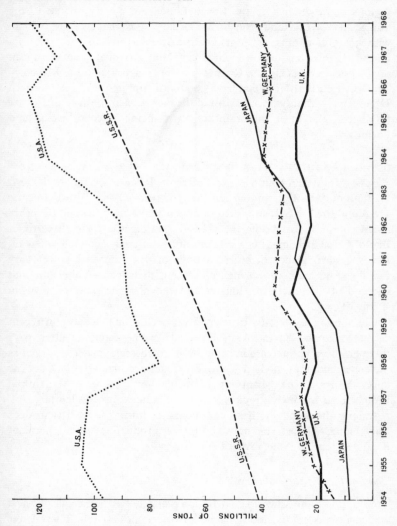

Fig. 25. Growth of Crude Steel Output of Five Major Producers, 1954-68

COMECON. This economic grouping is made up of the countries of Eastern Europe plus the USSR. In 1968 it produced 140 million tons, and the USSR alone accounted for 106 millions of this. The main regions of production in the Soviet Union are closely related to the availability of coal and iron ore. The largest is the Ukraine, which, with 30 million tons, accounts for nearly one-third of the country's output. It relies mainly on Donbas coal, and Krivoi Rog and Crimean ores. Other centres are the Kuznetsk basin (Kuzbas) and the Moscow–Tula district, both of which have good coal supplies, and the southern Ural region with its iron ore. Most of the Eastern European countries are producers, the most important of them being Czechoslovakia and Poland.

OTHER PRODUCERS. Most of the remaining 15 per cent comes from about half a dozen countries, and of these Japan is by far the largest. With an output of 67 million tons in 1968 it now comes third after the USA and the USSR, and turns out eight times more than all the other Asian countries (excluding the USSR) put together, and three times that of Great Britain. It is a sort of outpost of advanced technology on Asia's eastern seaboard, and has built up its industrial power very rapidly. The main producing centres are the Tokyo–Yokohama and Osaka–Kobe districts of Honshu and the northern part of Kyushu (Plate VI).

China has considerably developed its steelmaking capacity in recent years. Since the 'Great Leap Forward' in the economy after 1958 there has been an increase in smelting in small-scale furnaces as well as the construction of modern plant. The main producing regions are the lower Yangste, the Shantung peninsula and southern Manchuria. India's main producing region is in Bihar state west of Calcutta.

Among them the southern continents produce less steel than does Italy alone. Almost the only centres of production are in parts of Brazil, Argentina, South Africa and Australia.

The Location of the Industry

This highly confined world distribution is affected by numerous physical and economic factors, and by some historical ones as well. These latter are of special significance in an industry such as this with its large plant and costly installations. It is therefore particularly affected by 'geo-graphical inertia', which is to say that its location responds only slowly to changes in things such as supplies of raw materials and markets.

The most important locational factors can be summarised as follows:

FUEL SUPPLIES. Throughout most of the last century the presence of coal supplies was the most important single factor in the location of plant, and the bulk of the industry was therefore located either on or very near the coalfields. There were a number of causes for this.

(a) On account of its bulk in relation to its value, it was a difficult and costly item to transport very far.

(b) In the smelting process larger quantities of coal were needed than of iron ore, and it was therefore more economical that ore should be transported to the coal rather than vice versa. In 1800 as much as 6 tons of coal were needed to smelt 1 ton of iron.

(c) The carboniferous strata usually contain limestone and some iron as well.

Today such considerations as these no longer exercise anything like the influence over the industry which they have done in the past. The transport of coal is now far easier, and due to the greater efficiency of the process only about $1\frac{1}{4}$ tons of coal is needed to each ton of iron smelted. In addition to this electric furnaces have now become common for the making of special steels. The coal-measure ores are now little used, although limestone is still quarried in the vicinity of the coal. Yet the location of the coking coal supplies must still be taken into account, and some of the largest steel industries, such as those of the Ruhr and Pittsburgh, are situated on them. Even where, as in South Wales, the bulk of the industry has now migrated off the coalfield, its new location owes more to coal than to anything else.

IRON ORE. When the black and clay band ores were in general use, their existence further reinforced the value of coalfield sites. Now the iron ore is invariably situated away from the coal, and transport is necessary. At first it was the iron ore which was always transported, both because more coal was needed and because the heavy industry was already on the coalfields. By the end of the nineteenth century the orefields themselves had become the sites of much new development, especially when the ore was low grade and therefore costly to transport.

One of the best known of the orefield regions is Lorraine. Much of this region's fuel comes from the Ruhr, and the coal is moved along the Rhine waterway. The completion of the Moselle canalisation in 1964 further increased the ease and cheapness of this trade.

INTERMEDIATE LOCATIONS. Very often it is found preferable to transport both the coal and the iron ore some distance towards one another. In this case the industry is away from its supplies, but in a good location for communications. The new coastal sites at Dunkirk and Ijmuiden are of this type, since they can take advantage of interior coal supplies and the imported ore.

LABOUR SUPPLY. An adequate labour force must be available, preferably one skilled in the various aspects of the work. This factor encourages the industry to remain in the same vicinity, or at least to move mainly to areas which already have industrial traditions.

MARKETS. The major markets for iron and steel and their products are the general manufacturing districts. As the transport of the raw materials has become easier, so more large plants are being situated near to the markets, or at least in positions with good communications to them. Examples of this are found in Japan, where some of the largest producers are in the general industrial areas around Tokyo and Osaka.

SCRAP METAL. In areas where scrap is plentiful it is very attractive to the steelmakers. It is economic because there is no preliminary smelting, and it can be taken straight to the steelworks. The largest quantities of scrap are naturally found at the markets, and so this exercises an influence similar to that of the markets themselves.

In the light of these factors, we will now consider in more detail the steel industries of Great Britain and the United States.

Great Britain

It was in Great Britain that many of the inventions were made which first enabled the development of modern industry. The aggregate of these is referred to as the 'Industrial Revolution', and it got under way at the end of the eighteenth century. Britain's lead was the result of her ample raw materials together with the favourable economic climate of

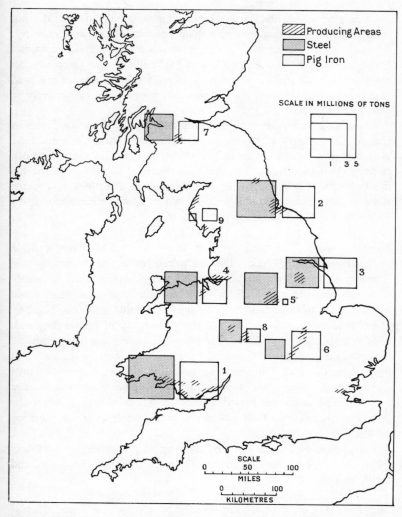

Fig. 26. Great Britain. Iron and Steel Production by Region. 1. South Wales. 2. The North-East. 3. Lincolnshire. 4. South Lancashire–North Wales. 5. Sheffield District. 6. East Midlands. 7. Central Scotland. 8. West Midlands. 9. North-West. (Numbers refer to squares to left of them)

the time, and as a result she was in the forefront of industrial nations throughout the last century.

Until after 1870 Britain was producing over half the world's pig iron, which was at that time the main product of the iron industry. By 1913 this had fallen to 12 per cent (10 million tons) and Britain had been overtaken by the United States (31 million) and Germany (17 million). In 1968 this country produced 16·7 million tons of pig, and 26·3 million tons of steel, 4·3 per cent and 5·5 per cent respectively of world output.

The coalfields and their neighbourhoods became the most favoured sites for the industry at the end of the eighteenth century, because here coal, limestone and ore were found together. Since the late nineteenth century the concentration on them has become far less, and the industry has steadily been moving towards counter-attractions. At present there are five main producing regions which among them account for 80 per cent of the nation's output (Fig. 26).

SOUTH WALES. The 'steel coast' of South Wales is the largest single producing area in Britain. The main centres are the Llanelly and Swansea districts, Port Talbot, Cardiff and Newport. Fuel is readily obtained from the coalfield immediately to the north, and high-grade ore is shipped from Canada, North Africa and South America (Fig. 27). Other favourable factors here are the availability of ample flat land, good transport, a large labour supply and markets for the products. The most important specialisations are on strip steel in the east and tin-plate in the west. This region accounts for 95 per cent of Britain's tinplate production; other non-ferrous metals notably zinc and copper are also used. This industry has evolved out of the time when the Swansea district was the country's main smelter of non-ferrous metals.[1]

Tin-plate is used mainly in food canning, and the various rolled steel sheets find ready markets in the industries of the Midlands and South-east.

THE NORTH-EAST COAST. The main producing area is Tees-side, and Middlesbrough is its centre. It grew to importance when the Cleveland

[1] It needs large water supplies, and facilities for importing raw materials, and both of these requirements are satisfied in the area.

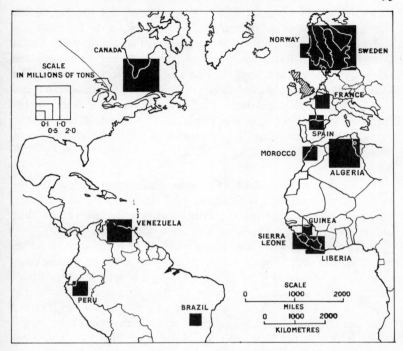

Fig. 27. Sources of Imports of Iron Ore into the United Kingdom

ores were brought into use after 1850, but the working of these ceased in 1964. It is well situated to obtain coking coal from the Durham area, and Swedish and other ores can be easily imported. The district specialises in heavy steel products for the North-East industrial region, the largest of its markets being the shipbuilding and engineering industries. Some iron and steel is still produced on the Durham coalfield, a relic of the days when the area was of considerable importance.

THE EAST MIDLANDS. This area now produces almost all the British output of iron ore (Fig. 12), and a large iron and steel industry has grown up around it. The main centres are Scunthorpe, Corby and Kettering, and there is a considerable output of pig iron for heavy equipment. The coal supplies come mostly from the York–Derby–Notts and Midland coalfields.

THE SHEFFIELD REGION. Unlike South Wales and the North-East where the centres of the industry are now coastal, in the Sheffield area steel production has remained firmly implanted on the coalfield. This is largely because it has stuck closely to its biggest and most consistent market, the cutlery industry. Pig iron and heavy steel are made in the Rother valley to the east, and then sent to Sheffield to be converted into the high-quality steels needed. A high proportion of scrap is used in the furnaces, and much pig iron is imported to be resmelted. The steel furnaces are generally small, and there is a large number of electric ones.

THE LANARKSHIRE REGION. The main centre of production is here located to the south-east of Glasgow. Good quality local coal is present, but ore has to be imported. The largest markets are the shipbuilding and marine engineering industries of Clydeside.

Smaller iron and steel industries are also to be found in many other areas. Most of the coalfields still do at least some smelting, and in many cases works have been sited on them to help alleviate the employment situation. This was one of the reasons for the site of the large integrated plant built at Ebbw Vale in the 1930s in an area which was a hundred years ago Britain's largest iron producer. South Lancashire, North Wales, south Staffordshire and the North-West also have a sizeable output, and the last region benefits from its proximity to the haematite ores.

Modern Trends

Three important developments have been taking place in the geography of the industry in the last twenty years. (1) The average size of the plants has been getting larger, and their numbers smaller. Most of those constructed since 1945 are integrated, and their sites have had to be carefully chosen to ensure the maximum advantage. (2) Production has increased most rapidly in the steel areas which serve expanding industries. The most rapidly expanding industrial areas are those of the Midlands and the South, and this has most benefited the South Wales and East Midland steel areas. In the North and in Scotland overall growth has been much slower, and this has had repercussions on the iron and steel industries of Tees-side and Lanarkshire. (3) The markets have been exercising a greater influence on the siting of new plants. In South Wales, for instance, the greatest developments, apart from tinplate, have been in the east at sites which are very convenient for sending the steel to the consumers. In South Staffordshire production has been increasing recently after a long period of decline, and this can be attributed to the large adjacent markets and supplies of scrap metal.

North America

This continent shows the operation of locating factors very well because it is for the most part a single economic unit, unlike Europe with its artificial barriers to trade. The main centres of the industry are in the north-east of the United States, where so much of the country's economic strength lies, and in parts of southern Canada (Fig. 28). The following are the main regional groupings.

THE PITTSBURGH DISTRICT. Although this is the most important single region, its production has not of late increased as rapidly as that of many others. It was in the 1860s that it soared to prominence, and by the end of the century it was turning out some 40 per cent of the nation's iron and steel. The so-called 'Pittsburgh Plus' system of prices ensured for its firms a large measure of control over the American industry until the 1920s. Its greatest assets are the presence of high-grade coking coal and good transport facilities for bringing in ore and moving heavy materials. It is also in a very central location in relation to America's manufacturing quadrilateral (p. 108).

THE LAKESIDES. Here the most important steel towns are along the southern shores of Lakes Michigan and Erie. They include Gary, Detroit, Toledo, Cleveland and Buffalo. The Superior iron ores in transit via the Lakes for Pittsburgh have to be unloaded at the Erie ports, so in the later nineteenth century it was found economic to bring down Appalachian coal for smelting at the lakesides. The Michigan producers used to be supplied with their coal from the East Interior field, but most of it is now higher-grade coal which comes from West Virginia. In recent years over 60 million tons of ore per annum have been transported eastwards, but now the supplies of Superior haematites are beginning to run down. They are being supplemented

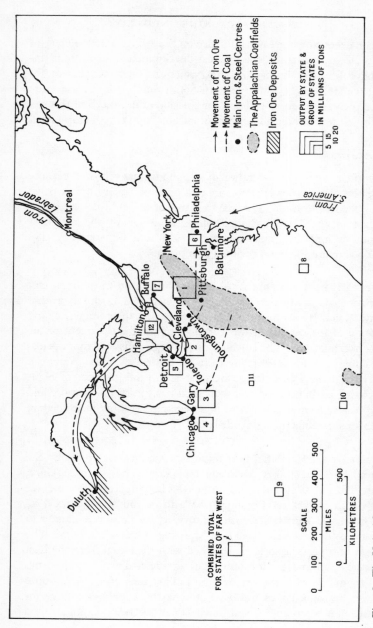

Fig. 28. The United States and Canada. Iron and Steel Production. By states and state groups. 1. Pennsylvania. 2. Ohio. 3. Indiana. 4. Illinois. 5. Michigan. 6. New Jersey–Delaware–Maryland. 7. New York. 8. South-East Seaboard. 9. Texas–Oklahoma. 10. Mississippi Valley. 11. Kentucky. 12. Canada

Movement of Iron Ore
Movement of Coal
Main Iron & Steel Centres
The Appalachian Coalfields
Iron Ore Deposits

OUTPUT BY STATE & GROUP OF STATES IN MILLIONS OF TONS
5   10   15   20

SCALE
MILES
0   100   200   300   400   500
KILOMETRES
0   500

COMBINED TOTAL FOR STATES OF FAR WEST

From Labrador
Montreal
Duluth
Buffalo
Hamilton
Detroit
Cleveland
Chicago
Gary
Toledo
Youngstown
Pittsburgh
New York
Philadelphia
Baltimore
From S. America

by increasing quantities of Labrador ores, which can be brought by the St Lawrence Seaway. Production is closely tailored to meet the needs of the great Mid-West manufacturing industries.

Closely related to this steelmaking complex is Canada's main centre, the Toronto–Hamilton district. This makes full use of the water transport provided by the St Lawrence–Lakes system. Much ore comes from Labrador, and coal is brought in via the Welland canal from the United States, as well as from the coalfields of Canada's Maritime Provinces.

THE OREFIELDS. It was not until 1915 that an iron and steel industry was first established at Duluth making use of coal shipped as a return cargo from the Pittsburgh district. The industry here has failed to expand much because of the long distances involved, and the limited markets in the vicinity for its products.

THE MIDDLE ATLANTIC SEABOARD. There is a large concentration of the industry here, particularly in the Baltimore and Philadelphia districts. Appalachian coal and limestone are used, and iron ore is imported from South America and Canada. Water transport is again of great importance for the conveyance of the heavy materials. This region benefits from its proximity to the large eastern market, and in recent years its growth has been extremely rapid (Plate IV).

THE SOUTHERN APPALACHIANS. Here the industry is centred on the Birmingham area, which has adjacent supplies of coal, ore and limestone. In spite of these unrivalled advantages, its growth has been handicapped by the smallness of the southern market. This is now growing, and the area is producing a variety of steel products including wire and piping. There is now a danger that the local raw materials will prove to be insufficient, and in that case the distances from water will prove a disadvantage.

THE WEST. Most of the largest western cities produce steel, although the area is poor in the necessary raw materials. Its development has been in response to the rapid growth of the region's industries, and to government inducements so as to lessen the excessive concentration in the north-east.

CEMENT AND ALLIED INDUSTRIES

Cement in its various forms is one of the most important of all the materials used by the construction industries. With improved technology, products such as concrete which are made from it are now even replacing metals for many purposes. Cement and concrete are no less versatile than are steels, and a large range of different types are now available with various degrees of hardness, durability and tensility. Cement is traditionally used in the making of buildings and roads, but it has now become well established in the construction of bridges, dams and port installations, as well as for casting into pipes and as the basis of many new building techniques. The material can be given added strength by inserting steel wiring through it.

There are many different sorts of cement, and each is made for its own particular qualities. The three most important in current use are the following:

PORTLAND CEMENT. This is the most widely used, and it is made by fusing together two substances, one calcareous and one argillaceous (clay) with the addition of gypsum. The best calcareous materials are either chalk or limestone, and many different sorts of clay can be used, provided they have the right mineral composition. In some cases the limestone itself may contain sufficient clay, or the clay may be lime-rich. In such cases it may be possible to use this material alone, or with very little additive. The process consists of mixing together the constituents, generally in water, and then fusing them at high temperatures. The material which results from this is known as 'clinker' and it is then ground down to a powder before it can be used.

RAPID HARDENING CEMENT. The process is exactly the same, but the size of the grind is varied so as to give the qualities required.

HIGH ALUMINA CEMENT. This is made by the fusion of lime with a material of high alumina content. This is generally bauxite, and the result is a very strong cement which is very resistant to heat and corrosion by acids.

Other materials, notably slag and china clay, can be used to make cement with particular qualities.

RIVER MEDWAY

V. Cement plants at North Halling, Kent. Raw materials are quarried near at hand (1) and coal for the kilns is brought in by rail (2). Cement is despatched by rail and road (2 and 3) to the surrounding counties and the London area. Cement for export is taken along the Medway from the jetty (4) in small ships for delivery to nearby countries or for transhipment to ocean-going vessels.

OSAKA BAY

VI. The waterside at Kobe, Japan, has a great number of industrial activities crowded into a small area. In the foreground are the shipbuilding and repairing yards (1), while across the river carriers discharge imported ore to feed the blast furnaces (2) and mills (3) of an integrated·iron and steel plant. In the middle distance is an oil refinery (4) and behind this the general cargo docks (5). (Compare this with Plate 2.)

World Production

World production of cement is now over 500 million tons. Of this approaching 50 per cent comes from Western Europe and North America (Fig. 29), and another 30 per cent from the USSR and the countries of East and South-East Asia. This contrasts with the situation in 1954 when the former countries were producing 67 per cent of the world's output and the latter just over 20 per cent. Appreciable quantities are also being produced in South America, South Africa, Australia and the Middle East.

Between 1954 and 1962 world production rose by 87 per cent, and the most rapid increases have been occurring in the countries of Eastern Europe and Asia. For instance, over this period the production of the USSR rose from 19 million to 57·3 million tons, an increase of 195 per cent, while that of Japan rose by 170 per cent from 10·7 millions to 28·8 millions. At the same time United States production rose from 46·4 to 59·9 (27 per cent). Between 1962 and 1968 world production increased by a further 40 per cent, amongst the largest national increases being those of Japan with 62 per cent and the USSR with 52 per cent. At the same time Western European output went up by 35 per cent and that of the United States by 10 per cent.

Production in Western Europe

In 1968 the output of this region was 160 million tons, nearly one-third that of the world. The four largest producers are, in order of importance, West Germany, Italy, France and the United Kingdom, and of the smaller producers the largest are Spain, Austria, Belgium and Switzerland. The rate of production increase has varied considerably in the last few years, this depending largely on the economic development in the country, and the part concrete has played in this. Concrete has been of particular importance in those countries with large building programmes, and also in those where the iron and steel industry is insufficient to meet current needs and there has been an impetus to use cement products as substitutes. Of the four largest European producers, the greatest growth in output has been Italy's, with an increase of 127 per cent between 1954 and 1962, and a further 50 per cent between 1962 and 1968. That of the United Kingdom was 17 per cent between 1954 and 1962, but increased to 28 per cent between 1962 and 1968.

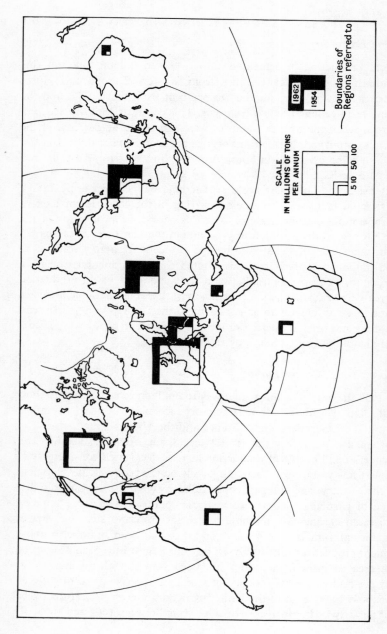

Fig. 29. World Production of Cement by Region, 1954 and 1962

Production is most highly concentrated in those localities which possess the best raw materials, and at the same time have good facilities for transporting them to the main consuming areas. The most important centre in France is the Boulonnais which, with its varied geological structure, contains the necessary raw materials very close at hand. Parts of the French Alps with their large limestone resources are also of considerable importance. In Germany the middle and lower Rhinelands

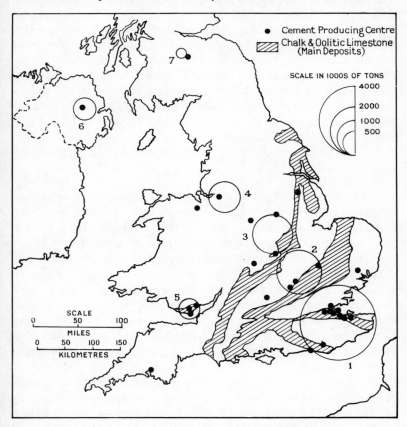

Fig. 30. Production of Cement in the United Kingdom. 1. Thames–Weald Region. 2. South-East Midlands. 3. East Midlands. 4. South Lancashire–North Wales. 5. South Wales and the West. 6. Northern Ireland. 7. Scotland

have the raw materials and coal, and are best located for transport. Italy is very rich in limestone, and the main centres are in the north, and in the Rome–Naples vicinity. Other localities of importance in Western Europe are the Swiss Alps and central Belgium.

Production in Great Britain

The most important producing areas in Great Britain are in the south, stretching in a broad belt from the Mersey to the Thames (Fig. 30). By far the greatest concentration lies around the lower Thames estuary, which accounts for about one-third of the nation's total. The most important centres are Grays, Northfleet and Cliffe, together with the lower Medway region in the vicinity of Rochester. In the East Midlands, the vicinities of Oxford, Luton, Cambridge and Rugby all have a considerable output. The other parts of the country where the industry is of importance are South Wales (especially Cardiff) and the South Lancashire–North Wales region.

The following are the main factors which have influenced the industry's location:

THE PRESENCE OF THE RAW MATERIALS. Chalk outcrops in large quantities on the Chilterns and the Downs, and it accounts for 70 per cent of the calcareous material used by the British producers. Farther west are the oolitic limestones outcropping in a broad belt which stretches diagonally across the country from Dorset to Yorkshire. This is at its widest in the Cotswold hills of the centre. To supply the other main constituent, the intervening clay vales and the clay and mud from the London Basin have the necessary mineral content. It is these rocks, or rocks of the same age, which account for almost all the requirements of the cement industry. To use others would necessitate extraction, and this process could not be economic in the circumstances.

NEARNESS TO MARKETS. Since it is a bulky material of low value in proportion to its weight, cement needs cheap transport or nearness to the consuming areas. Although it is used throughout Britain, its largest markets are in the centre and south, and it is able to serve these with little difficulty.

GOOD TRANSPORT is needed both for the product and for the raw materials used in the making of it. The coastal and near coastal sites of the South-East enable coal for the furnaces to be brought in by sea, and cement can also be exported easily in the same way (Plate V).

World Trade

Despite its bulk, cement is exported in large quantities from many of the largest producers, in particular those of Western Europe. There is much trade among the European countries themselves, as well as considerable exporting to other parts of the world (Fig. 31). France

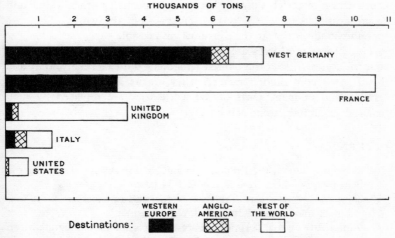

Fig. 31. Exports of Cement from Selected Countries

exports the most, over two-thirds of this being destined for countries outside Western Europe, mainly in Africa. By contrast, the second largest of the exporters, West Germany, sends over three-quarters of its total to other Western European countries. The United Kingdom's trade pattern is similar to that of France, but on a much smaller scale.

In the last decade international trade has been steadily declining, due largely to increased home production in the importing countries.

Concrete

This is made by mixing the cement with an aggregate, a substance which gives the material body and added strength. The particular aggregate used will depend both on the qualities it is desired to produce, and the availability of particular materials in sufficient quantities. The most common aggregates are sand, gravel, crushed stone or brick, slag and pumice.

BRICKS

These are made from clay and shales, materials which have a very widespread distribution. Subject to there being adequate supplies of fuels, bricks can be manufactured in very many areas. However, like other construction materials they are heavy in proportion to their value, and so are costly to transport long distances from the works. They are therefore made as near to the consumers as possible.

The largest producers are the USSR and the Western European countries, in particular the United Kingdom, West Germany, Italy and Spain. As a construction material they are used less widely than is cement, and in many parts of the world they are replaced by such materials as timber, stone and concrete.

STUDENT WORK

1. Write an essay on the French iron and steel industry, explaining the main factors which have influenced its location.
2. Compare and contrast, in relation to fuel and raw materials, the iron and steel industries of Italy and West Germany.
3. Dunkirk, Bruges and Ijmuiden are the sites for new integrated iron and steel plants in the Common Market. With the aid of a sketch map, explain the advantages of these locations.
4. In the Ruhr heavy industrial area, the western part has lately been developing more rapidly than the eastern part. Suggest reasons for this.
5. What advantages has the South Wales steel industry derived from moving from the coalfields to the adjacent coast?
6. Evaluate the advantages and disadvantages of (a) London, (b) Glasgow and (c) Coventry as possible sites for a new integrated steel plant.
7. Write an essay on the importance of water transport in the iron and steel industry of North America.
8. What effects is the increasing United States dependence on foreign ores having, and likely to have, on the geography of the country's steel industry?

9. What advantages does Canada possess for the further expansion of her steel production?

10. What problems face the African countries in the establishment of iron and steel industries?

11. Write an account of the factors influencing the location of the iron and steel industry in the Soviet Union.

12. Suggest reasons for the following:
    (a) Pennsylvania is the largest producer of cement in the United States.
    (b) The Boulonnais region produces over half the cement made in France.
    (c) In recent years the cement output of Italy has been increasing far more rapidly than has that of the United Kingdom.

13. Attempt to explain why cement production in the Soviet Union and Eastern Europe is increasing more rapidly than that of the United States and Western Europe.

14. Write a comparative account of the building construction industries in Scandinavia and the United Kingdom, explaining the reasons for the differences you find.

Chapter 7

General Manufacturing Industry

GENERAL manufacture is the making of the vast range of materials and equipment which are needed in our complex modern way of life. These industries are dependent for many of their materials upon those we have been considering, and the bulk of them are highly concentrated into very limited areas.

MAIN MANUFACTURING REGIONS

The greatest concentration of manufacturing activity is in the temperate zone of the northern hemisphere, particularly between 30° and 60° North. Of greatest importance are Western Europe, north-east America and Japan, followed by western USSR, east-central Europe and California (Fig. 32). Each of these areas has its own characteristic industrial structure.

The American Manufacturing Quadrilateral

This area is the heartland of North America's industry. It stretches from the western shores of Lake Michigan through the Northern Appalachians and Canada's Lakes Peninsula to the Atlantic seaboard of the USA. There is considerable regional specialisation, with the west producing the greater part of the transport equipment, the north-east textiles and light engineering, and the south-east ships and chemicals.

Western Europe

Manufacturing here is less concentrated because of the large number of countries which duplicate one another's products. Movements towards greater political and economic unity, such as the Common Market,

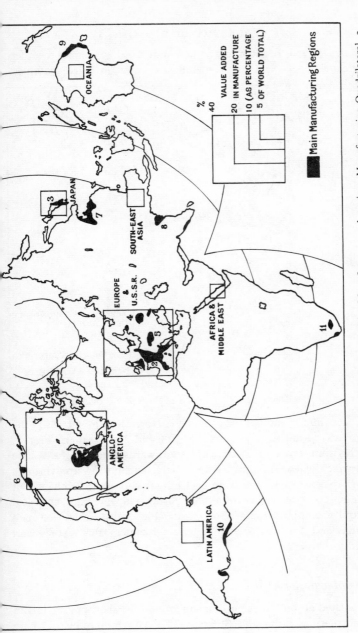

Fig. 32. The Main Manufacturing Regions, and Value Added by Manufacture. 1. American Manufacturing Quadrilateral. 2. Western Europe. 3. Japanese Manufacturing Belt. 4. Western U.S.S.R. 5. Eastern Europe. 6. California. 7. North-East China. 8. India. 9. South-East Australia. 10. South America. 11. South Africa

have, however, now begun to draw these individual economies together.
The greatest concentration of manufacturing is in those countries

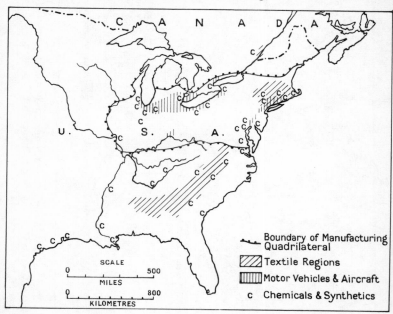

Fig. 33. The Manufacturing Region of Eastern North America

situated around the southern shores of the North Sea, in particular the
Low Countries, north-west Germany, England and northern France.
From this hub, tentacles stretch out southwards through the Rhône
corridor and Switzerland to northern Italy, and northwards through
Denmark to central Sweden. Manufacturing is very varied, and each of
the four largest countries makes motor vehicles, ships, textiles, chemical
and electrical equipment. There is considerable local specialisation such
as Switzerland for clocks and watches, Flanders for textiles and
Sheffield for cutlery.

Japanese Manufacturing Belt

This is located in southern Honshu, and around the shores of the inland
sea in northern Kyushu and Shikoku. The growth of industries here

has been very rapid, and is essentially a product of the present century. As a result of limited internal markets, there has been considerable emphasis on foreign trade, so tending to make the products more

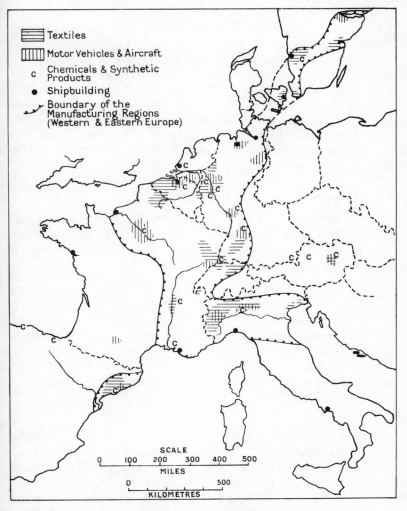

Fig. 34. The Major Manufacturing Region of Western Europe (excluding Great Britain)

specialist than in either of the other two areas. Of particular importance are wireless equipment, motor-cycles, cameras and textile fabrics.

West-central USSR

In proportion to its heavy industrial strength, both the quantity and variety of manufactured goods here are small. This is because of the weight which has been given to the rapid growth of heavy industry in the Five and Seven Year Plans. The most important goods are textiles, aircraft and chemicals. Partly as a result of the government's deliberate policy of decentralisation, the concentration is far less than in the other regions we have considered, but the Moscow region stands out as of paramount importance. The southern Urals and Ukraine have considerable manufactures, and there is steady development in the central Asian republics.

Eastern Europe

The adjacent parts of East Germany, northern Czechoslovakia and southern Poland form a large if discontinuous industrial area. The most developed branches of industry here are chemicals, textiles and heavy engineering.

Southern California

Industrial development here during the last quarter century has been among the most rapid in the world. It is closely allied economically to the north-east of the USA, and there is considerable assembly of components from the east into such things as motor vehicles and aircraft. Other industries are electrical equipment and food canning.

Other Regions

The rest of the world's manufacturing areas are of two sorts. There are those in the vanguard of the underdeveloped nations which are using local power and raw materials to industrialise rapidly. China and India are of this type, and characteristic industries are textiles, metals and construction materials. The centre of Chinese manufacturing is the north-east of the country, which is diversifying from silk and cotton goods to a wide range of equipment. In India, Bengal, Bihar and

Bombay are the most industrialised states with large textile and metal industries.

The other sort of industrial development is that of the more advanced nations situated away from the world's major industrial regions. The most important of these are Australia, South Africa, Brazil and Argentina. In Australia motor vehicles, chemicals and engineering are becoming more important, and there are similar although less striking developments in South Africa. Besides food processing and canning, the South American countries are now widening their industrial range to include a large range of consumer goods.

We shall now consider the distribution of a selection of individual industries.

SHIPBUILDING

Until the second half of the last century most ships were made of wood and powered by sail. They were small and, by modern standards, simple, so the dockyards could be situated at or near the ports they served. After 1850 there was a revolution which replaced timber and sail by iron and steam. In 1850 only 10 per cent of tonnage constructed was of iron, while by 1880 this had risen to 95 per cent.

These great technical changes had their repercussions on the geography of the industry, concentrating it into those areas most suitable for the construction of the new vessels. The main requirements were (1) ample supplies of iron and marine engineering products; (2) deep water and space for the shipyards; and (3) a market for the vessels.

Well into the present century these conditions were best fulfilled in Britain, which was overwhelmingly the world's greatest shipbuilder. In 1905 the United Kingdom built 1·9 out of the world's 3·3 million tons, while Germany, her nearest rival, accounted for only a quarter of that amount. The market served was the immense British merchant fleet, together with the fleets of the other main trading nations.

Throughout the present century the proportion of the world's ships coming from British yards has steadily diminished, and in 1964 it represented only 10 per cent of world output. In 1968 Britain's output was just under one million tons and this represented only 5 per cent of the total for that year. This decline has many causes, including the

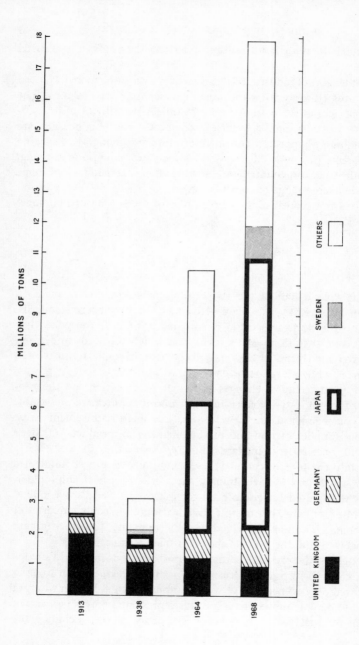

Fig. 35. The World's Major Shipbuilding Nations, 1913, 1938, 1964 and 1968

growth of the industry in other countries which were late starters. In addition to this, British production itself has been fluctuating considerably, and has been decreasing since 1957 (Fig. 35).

The same areas in the United Kingdom have remained shipbuilding centres for the best part of a century. The most important of these are the estuaries of the Clyde, Tyne, Tees, Wear and Mersey, together with Belfast Lough and Barrow-in-Furness. The most important of these is the Clyde, which averages about a quarter of the total output. It has traditionally specialised in large passenger vessels, the three 'Queens' being among its most renowned products. The deep water of the Clyde estuary, the heavy industry above Glasgow and the absence of any strong competitors for the available space were strong inducements to the establishment of shipbuilding here, and they remain so today. In the other regions, similar combinations of circumstances still act to their advantage (Fig. 40).

The other most important shipbuilding countries are Japan, Germany and Sweden, all of which have increased their output since 1945. By far the most spectacular increase has been that of Japan, which since 1955 has been the world's leading shipbuilder. Over the decade previous to 1964 her output increased tenfold to 4·1 million tons, 40 per cent of the world's total. By 1968 it had more than doubled to 8·7 million tons, which was now almost exactly a half that of the world. Japan's position in this respect is now very similar to that of Britain at the beginning of the twentieth century. The main yards are in the south of the country at such sites as Yokohama, Osaka and Hiroshima. Here good locations and a plentiful cheap labour supply are available, together with the steel and engineering materials needed. Further stimulus to construction is given by the continued increase in Japan's external trade, with the consequent need for merchant vessels. Unlike conditions in Britain, Japanese shipbuilding is not an 'old' industry having to expend much time and energy on modernisation, but a new one developed on contemporary lines and with a great capacity for rapid and large scale production.

Western Europe, which dominated world shipbuilding for over a century has now been overtaken by Japan. In 1964 it was responsible for a half of the tonnage launched, but by 1968 this was down to 37 per cent. About two-thirds of its output is from the 'Big Three' – Germany, Sweden and Britain.

By contrast, both the United States and the Soviet Union are well down the list as builders of merchant vessels. In both of them maritime trade is of much less significance, and in the case of the United States there is competition from well-organised foreign yards to supply them with vessels.

CHEMICALS

The chemical industries are concerned with changing the actual compositions of raw materials so as to separate out the elements, or combine them to form new substances. The products of this branch of industry are very diverse, and are used in a wide range of other industries. There are two categories of chemical manufacture: heavy chemicals and chemical products.

Heavy Chemicals

This is the preparation of materials which are to be used for chemical products or for other industrial processes. The two major branches are the production of acids and of alkalis. Sulphuric, hydrochloric and nitric acid are of importance in many heavy and light industrial processes. Sulphuric acid can be made from iron pyrites or sulphur, and it is used in making other acids. The two principal alkalis are caustic soda and carbonate of soda made from common salt. Nitrogen can be extracted from the air, and potash is obtained either from vegetation or from potassium salts. Both coal and petroleum have a large number of by-products used chemically. The destructive distillation of coal produces ammonia, and synthetic materials, including dyes, are made from coal tar.

Chemical Products

Some of the best-known chemical products are soap, detergents, fertilisers, insecticides, dyes, paint and glass. Soap is a compound of caustic soda, potash and fat or oil, and various detergents use a similar base, with other solvent or abrasive substances added. Glass is made from the fusing of sand and caustic soda in great heat. Fertilisers contain many chemicals designed to rejuvenate the soil, the most important of these being phosphates, nitrates and potash. Coal tar or aniline dyes have now come to be universally used instead of vegetable ones, and coal also provides a large number of other by-products.

MAN-MADE FIBRES. During the last twenty years a great new range of chemical products have been revolutionising many aspects of industry. These have been labelled 'synthetics', although in fact they are no more synthetic than most chemical materials already used. What is revolutionary about them is that they are ways of making artificially things which have previously been obtained from natural sources. The most significant ones are synthetic rubber, artificial fibres and plastics. The rubber is made from petroleum, and it now accounts for a half of all that used in industry (see p. 41 and table on p. 137).

The fibres are of two sorts: cellulose and true synthetics. Cellulosics have an organic base, the most usual materials being wood pulp or cotton linters. The wood pulp is dissolved in caustic soda to make viscose, while cotton linters are more suited to being dissolved in a mixture of acetic and sulphuric acid, so making acetate. These cellulosics make up the larger part of man-made fibre production, and are sometimes known by the general name of 'rayon'. The non-cellulosics have a coal tar or petroleum base. Nylon is made from the former, and polyester from the latter, while acrylic is a derivative both of oil refining and of coal carbonisation. There is a comparable distinction between the two different types of plastics, these being made in much the same way.

Main Chemical Producers

Although the production of chemicals is not confined to limited areas as is the case with shipbuilding, nevertheless there are many geographical requirements. Those areas having local supplies of salt and other minerals, together with coal, are especially suitable, and since there have to be some imports, coastal or river sites are the most economic. It is in Germany that some of the most notable developments in the modern chemical industry have taken place, especially in the fields of dyes, synthetics and explosives. These developments owe much to the country's wealth of potassium and common salt, together with its immense coal and lignite reserves. The wars of the earlier part of the

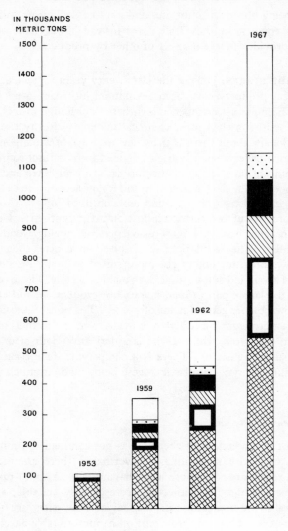

Fig. 36. Production of Non-Cellulosic Continuous Fibres in the Largest
Producers and the USSR

century also encouraged the Germans to attempt to make artificially those substances which they might not be able to import, and great strides were made in the production of synthetic rubber and, to a lesser extent, synthetic petrol.

The main centres of the German industry today are in a belt between the northern plain and the central mountains. It is here that the main reserves of the necessary raw materials are found. In the lower Rhineland, Krefeld and Leverkusen are known for their aniline dyes, and Düren for its glass. Ruhr coal and Ville lignite are used, and nearness to the Rhine makes the area suitable for the import of heavy chemicals. Farther east at Merseburg and Leuna there are large plants making fertiliser and explosives.

In Great Britain the coasts are the most economical locations for many branches of the industry because of the large imports which have to be made. Important centres are Merseyside, the north-east coast and the Severn estuary. Of these Merseyside is the oldest and most diverse. It is situated between the Lancashire coalfield to the north and the Cheshire saltfield to the south, and is noted for its soap, glass, fertiliser and dyes.

The greatest chemical producer in the world is the United States. This country has large reserves of most of the necessary raw materials, and the industry is widespread throughout the east of the country. Japan has developed its industry since 1945, and in many branches is now second only to the United States. She is motivated in this by the lack of many essential raw materials which can be produced synthetically by her chemical industry, and is helped by the large home production of sulphur and salt. The USSR produces large quantities of fertiliser and explosives, but many aspects of the industry have been neglected. As a result of the rise in home consumption a great deal of attention is now being given to this Soviet industry. Other European countries have large chemical industries, the most important being those of Italy, France and Sweden, in all of which the production of synthetic substances is increasing rapidly.

TEXTILES

The textile industry is one of long duration in the established centres of industry, where it has become concentrated into a number of specialist regions. During the present century the degree of concentration has been decreased by expansion both within and outside the old industrial areas, and the industry is now almost more widespread than any other.

At the present day the regions where textiles are manufactured are of two sorts. First there are the old-established ones in Europe and North America, situated within the industrial parts of those continents. These depend for most of their raw materials on imports into the regions, and they have their largest markets near at hand. Then there are the newer manufacturing areas in Asia, Africa and South America, which by contrast have grown up near to supplies of raw materials. In the United States the old and the new are found in different parts of the country, and this contributes to the nation's economic power.

Europe

The European textile industry is large and varied, and encompasses the spinning and weaving of cotton, wool, flax, silk and man-made fibres, and the making of these materials into clothing and cloth for other purposes. The greater part of this manufacture is still concentrated into a very few regions, the most important of which are the following:

FLANDERS. This includes the area stretching from north-east France into western Belgium, and has the longest history of any textile region in northern Europe. The most important towns are Lille, Tourcoing, Roubaix, Ghent and Bruges, and cotton, wool and flax are the main fibres used. Many of the factors which encouraged the establishment of the industry here have long since ceased to be of any importance. They include the fact that until the seventeenth century England was Europe's 'Australia', and Flanders was well situated geographically to receive imports of wool from it. At present, the locally produced flax and the soft water, together with the coalfield slightly to the south, all contribute to its suitability.

LOWER GERMAN RHINELANDS. The main centres of West Germany's most important area of production are clustered on either side of the Rhine. To the east are Wuppertal, Elberfeld and Barmen, strung out along a small tributary stream, and on the west Mönchen-Gladbach,

Krefeld and Aachen. The reasons for the actual sites of manufacture are largely historical. The local wool, together with water for power and washing, were important reasons, but of these only the soft water is now an asset. However, the Ruhr coalfield nearby supplies power, bleaching agents and dyestuffs. Besides this, the great concentration of population in the region, together with the excellent facilities for importing raw materials, have been further advantages.

NORTHERN ENGLAND. The main centres of the textile industry here are around the southern flanks of the Pennines and in the north Midlands. It is considered in more detail below.

NORTHERN ITALY. The industry here is located in the western part of the Po basin, and centres on Milan and Turin. All types of textile materials are made, but in recent years the making of wool and man-made fibre materials has been expanding most rapidly. The silk industry uses the local product (p. 35) and hydro-electric power from the Alps has considerably aided growth.

NORTH-EAST SPAIN. The industry is largely confined to the province of Catalonia, and centres on the great industrial city of Barcelona. It originally made use of the large local wool supplies, but now cotton is the most important raw material. Use is being made of the small home cotton output.

EASTERN EUROPE. Grouped around the mountains of East Germany, southern Poland and northern Czechoslovakia are a number of very important textile regions. Notable centres are Karl Marx Stadt (Chemnitz), Lodz, Moravska Ostrava and Brno. As with West Germany, there is a historical reason for the sites of industry, but coalfields and local markets have helped their modern expansion.

The British Textile Industry

The oldest of the modern textile regions in Western Europe are situated around the south Pennines. It was here in the late eighteenth century that the industry was first mechanised, through the invention of the spinning 'Jenny', so opening the way to mass production of fabrics. The main fibres used today are wool, cotton, silk and synthetics. The greater part of the wool spinning and weaving is found in the West Riding of Yorkshire, and that of cotton on the other side of the Pennines in south Lancashire. At the time of the growth of the textile industry here, both sides were suitable for woollens, having water power, soft water, local wool and – to be used slightly later – plenty of coal. The water supplies and high humidity of northern England made the same regions equally suitable for cotton. However, in the nineteenth century cotton became a 'boom' industry, and for mass production the western side of the mountains proved best. This was because almost all supplies of raw cotton came from the United States, and, on account of shorter distance and good port facilities, Liverpool was the best importing point. This advantage, inherent in Lancashire's position, was reinforced by two man-made ones. In 1894 the Manchester Ship Canal was completed, and this thirty-five-mile-long waterway from Eastham Locks to Salford enabled raw materials to be brought straight into the heart of the cotton region. Secondly, there was the growth of the Merseyside chemical industry, providing the dyes and other materials needed for the cotton goods.

Today the cotton region is still located where it grew up, on either side of the Rossendale forest. The curious division, unknown elsewhere, into the spinning district to the south and the weaving to the north still remains. This undoubtedly owes its origin to the economic circumstances of the last century which encouraged the weavers to move out to cheaper land and more space north of Rossendale, but it has come through to the present as a 'built in' part of the industry's geography, which is difficult to explain by reference to the physical background alone. Manchester is the centre for finishing and the making of cotton piece goods. The industry is now but a shadow of its former self, as a result of changes which are similar to those which have affected so many of the older industrial districts. Consumption of raw cotton in 1964 had shrunk to just over 233,000 tons, less than a quarter that of 1913, and by 1968 it was down further to 175,000 tons. In 1913 Lancashire exported 6,000 million square yards (5,000 million square metres) of cotton cloth, which was three and a half times its total production in 1960, and eight times its output in 1968. Within this much smaller framework the industry is now more prosperous than it has been for many years. Considerable quantities of man-made fibre are now used within the region, both alongside and in conjunction with the cotton, and many new industries, particularly engineering, have been introduced.

The woollen region of Yorkshire centres upon the Aire and Calder valleys, having grown up highly confined to those areas possessing soft water. The concentration of wool here is only slightly less than that of cotton across the Pennines, although local woollen industries remain in many other parts of Britain. The industry has remained prosperous, and there has been less contraction than in the case of cotton. There are many reasons for this, including the continued high demand for high quality woollens, and the smaller competition from foreign rivals. Synthetic fibres have also made less impact, and the process of adjustment has therefore been an easier one.

Besides these two great concentrations, textiles are produced in a number of other localities. Macclesfield is famous for its silk, Nottingham and Glasgow for lace and Dundee has a jute industry. London is important for all types of clothing.

The most recent and fastest growing additions to the British industry, as also to those of many other countries, are the man-made fibres (p. 117). The manufacture of these is not tied to any particular locality, although there must be good transport facilities for the assembly of such raw materials as coal, petroleum and wood pulp. It is the chemical regions which supply the prepared raw materials, so North Wales, south Lancashire and the North-East have attracted the industry. Other important producing towns are Coventry and Pontypool.

Present European Production

The total output of cotton cloth in Western Europe in 1968 was 1·8 million tons, a considerable increase over the 1952 figure of a million. Production increased everywhere except in Scandinavia and the United Kingdom. The United Kingdom's share of Western Europe's production over this period decreased from 23 per cent to 15 per cent. At the same time that of West Germany declined from 16 per cent to 12 per cent, while the shares of France and Italy increased. Similarly the United Kingdom's share of woollen cloth output has declined. Although the number of installed spindles is still equal to three-quarters that of the whole of the Common Market, yet woollen cloth

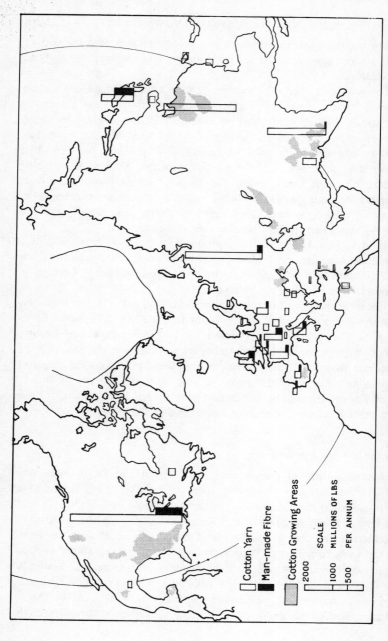

Fig. 37. Cotton Yarn and Man-made Fibre Production in the Industrial Countries of the Northern Hemisphere

production for 1962 was less than that of Italy alone. Similarly production of man-made fibres was greatest in Italy until recently, but she has now been overtaken by both Germany and Britain. Italy is the main silk fabric producer, followed by France, where production is concentrated in the Lyons area.

North America

Across the Atlantic is the world's second great textile region, which has a total output in many ways comparable to that of Europe. The main centres are New England, the Middle Atlantic region, the South and California. Of these southern New England is both the most varied and the oldest. It grew up in the early nineteenth century as a result of conditions similar to those found around the south Pennines. The large market provided by the east coast towns later added to the value of this location, although the absence of coal proved a disadvantage. This had to be imported by sea, and so drew the industry more towards the coasts. New York and its region are of special importance for clothing and silks (Fig. 33).

A more recent development has been the growth of the South as a textile producer. This is an obvious development since it is the source of most of America's raw cotton and has a large and cheap labour supply. With its growing market, this area is more favoured than New England, and its gain has been New England's loss. The introduction of man-made fibres has further increased its importance, since its wealth of local chemicals, petroleum and coal makes it very suitable for this new industry. More recently the growing of cotton in California has stimulated the textile manufacturing industry there also.

Meanwhile New England has continued to decline in importance and now contains only about 10 per cent of the cotton spindles in the United States. It remains of much greater significance in the woollen industry, although it now accounts for only 40 per cent of the woollen spindles. As in Lancashire, this decline has been compensated for by the introduction of other industries, such as light engineering and electrical equipment.

Other Manufacturers

Most of the other textile-producing areas are either at or near the sources of their raw materials. As a result of the relative simplicity of the manufacturing process, together with the local markets, the textile industry has been one of the easiest to introduce into developing countries. It can also be a convenient way of increasing the local use of home-produced fibres. This has encouraged large increases in the consumption of cotton in India, Pakistan, China and Egypt, to the disadvantage of the European textile exporters. The most developed of Europe's competitors is Japan, where large cotton, silk and man-made fibres industries are flourishing. The main centres are Tokyo, Yokohama, Osaka and Kobe. Although Japan is the world's second largest raw silk producer, she has no raw cotton, and, with imports of 800,000 tons per annum, is now the world's largest importer of this commodity.

TABLE 5. *Consumption of cotton*
(figures in 1,000 bales)

	UNITED KINGDOM	INDIA	JAPAN
1952	1,453	3,492	1,894
1963–4	1,065	5,250	3,164

World Production – Summary

The world production of all major textiles continues to rise, but the individual national productions of particular materials remain variable. The fastest increase has been in man-made fibres, which nearly trebled in production in the period between 1950 and 1963, bringing up their share of the market from 18 per cent to 26 per cent (Fig. 36). This still remained far below cotton's 65 per cent, but although cotton production went up, its share decreased. Production of textile materials continued to rise in recent years, but the proportions of cotton and synthetic fibres remained almost constant. Wool is of far less importance than cotton, with only one-seventh of its production. Its use is more restricted to fabrics for the temperate and cold belts. Its share of the market has been declining in recent years.

NEW INDUSTRIES

Although each of the groups of industries which have so far been considered have branches which display the most up-to-date tech-

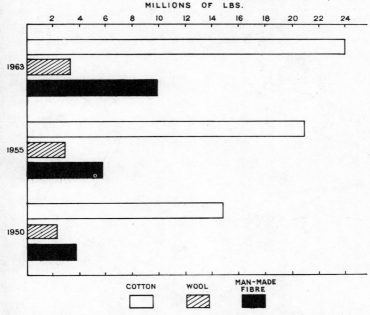

Fig. 38. Total World Output of Cotton, Wool, and Man-made Fibres
in 1950, 1955 and 1963

niques, they are all old industries which have been progressively modernised. There is, however, a large sector of industry which has grown up almost entirely during the present century, through the large-scale application of recent inventions. They include particularly motor vehicles, aircraft, television, radio receivers and electrical equipment. The greatest expansion of these industries first took place in the United States, where the combination of great resources with high standards of living made them practicable. More recently they have expanded in Europe, Japan and numerous other industrial areas. One of the most typical and important of them is the manufacture of motor vehicles.

Motor Vehicle Manufacture

The internal-combustion engine was invented in the 1880s, but for long it was regarded as being no more than a toy, and not until the First World War were its possibilities for transport fully realised.

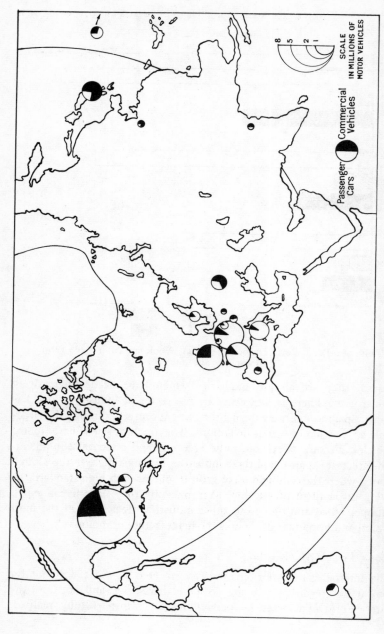

Fig. 39. World Motor Vehicle Output by Country (Brazil and Argentina are shown together; arrow denotes Australian production)

Since then the use of motor vehicles has steadily increased, and now in the advanced industrial countries they are the most widely used and flexible means of internal communication.

There are three important things to note about motor vehicles which help to explain the particular characteristics of their manufacture:

1. A very large proportion of the bodywork and engine is made out of metal, especially various steels and aluminium.

2. It is made up by the assembly of a great number of component parts ranging from such things as tyres and upholstery to electrical fittings.

3. It and its parts are all relatively light.

These three characteristics have had many effects on the geography of the industry. Since it uses large amounts of metal, it must be well placed to receive this from the producing regions. The steel used is mostly sheet, strip and alloy, and it can be moved longer distances economically than can the steels for heavy engineering. Again, since the industry is in the main a matter of assembling parts, it is best situated near to the areas where these are made. The third characteristic, its lightness, means that neither transport of parts nor of the finished products presents insuperable problems.

The best places to manufacture are therefore in the vicinity of heavy metal and general engineering regions, but not necessarily, or even preferably in the middle of them. This is because the giant newcomer needs plenty of space and good transport, and at the time of its development these conditions were not found in the older industrial areas.

REGIONS OF PRODUCTION. The greatest concentrations of manufacture are in North America and Western Europe, which are responsible for 85 per cent of the world output of 26 million vehicles. Of these, in 1968, 10·7 millions came from the United States alone, followed by West Germany with 3·1 millions, the United Kingdom with 2·2 millions and France with 2 millions. The total production of the Common Market countries was 7 millions, 65 per cent of the United States total. In 1954, Common Market production of 1·5 millions was only 22 per cent of the American for that year. For the whole of Western Europe the percentage has risen from 38 per cent to nearly 90 per cent over this period.

The world's largest motor-car industry is centred in Detroit at the western end of Lake Erie. The main American car firms have their headquarters in this city, and the manufacture of components extends over a wide area from Chicago to Buffalo. In recent years the high costs of labour and land, together with the opening up of new markets, has lessened the dominance of this region. Assembly is now carried out in the southern states and in California, and has spilled over the St Clair river to Windsor, and other parts of South Canada (Fig. 33).

In Western Europe, the degree of concentration is far less, as manufacture is carried out in so many different countries. The most important producing areas are the Paris region, northern Italy, the Lower Rhinelands, and the Midlands and South-East of England (Fig. 34).

PRODUCTION IN GREAT BRITAIN. The regions centring on London and Birmingham are the most important ones for motor vehicles. The main manufacturing towns include Birmingham, Coventry, Oxford, Luton and Dagenham. In these areas accessibility to component parts has been combined with ample space, good transport and a large market.

Coventry is the country's best example of a town which has grown up through this industry. At the end of the last century it was making bicycles, an industry sufficiently similar to motor-cars to make the transition quite an easy one. The nearby Black Country has traditionally specialised in small metal goods such as locks, keys, nuts, bolts and fittings, and so was able to supply components to the new industry. The central position of the town also meant that a variety of things can be assembled from farther afield, notably steels from South Wales and chemical products and textiles from the North. The low-lying land facilitating easy communications and the lack of any previous large-scale industry were additional factors which made it attractive to manufacturers. With all these advantages, Coventry is a 'classic' manufacturing city.

The locations of the other manufacturing towns vary considerably in their advantages and disadvantages, but central and south-east England has on the whole been an excellent area for the setting up of the motor industry. In the last few years government pressure has resulted in its spreading to other parts of the country, and new plants have been opened on Merseyside and in Renfrewshire (Fig. 40).

PRODUCTION IN THE REST OF THE WORLD. The greater part of the 17 per cent of the world's vehicles originating outside the two regions

VII. Motor vehicle plant at Turin, Northern Italy. This is built on a spacious and flat site which has little evidence of other industry. It is well located to receive hydro-electric power from the Alps (in the background) and to obtain parts from the surrounding industrial region.

VIII. Intensive farming in the North-East Polder of the Zuider Zee, Netherlands. The whole area is carefully planned, and every inch of available space is used up. Notice the high density of rural settlement and the use of canals for transport.

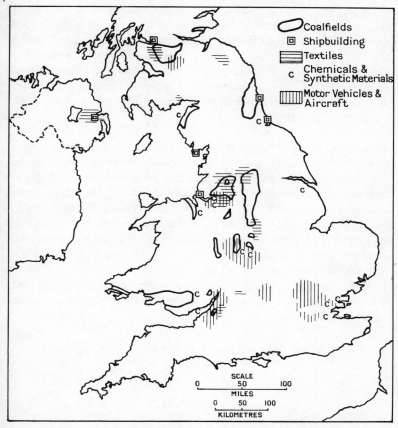

Fig. 40. The United Kingdom. Selected Industries

we have discussed come from Japan, the U S S R and Australia. Japan's increase has been spectacular, and between 1945 and 1964 it rose from 70,000 to 1·7 million. Between 1964 and 1968 there was a further increase to 4·1 million units, bringing it to second place among vehicle producing nations. Output of passenger cars and commercial vehicles is about equal while in the United States the latter is only a quarter of the former and in the European Community only one-tenth. Over this same period Australia's output increased only slightly less fast, from 54,000 to 500,000. Large numbers of the components are still imported, although the quantities made in Australia are steadily increasing. When one considers its immense industrial strength, the output of the USSR – 800,000 in 1968 – is small. This is in part due to the concentration on heavy industry which has already been mentioned, but it also results from the nature of the country itself. Its sheer size and the dispersal of its population, have caused motor vehicles to remain for the most part of only regional importance, the main lines of communication being by rail and air.

WORLD TRADE. The highly specialised nature of production, together with the great demand, has resulted in considerable international trade. The main exporters are the Western European countries, and all the main producers here export a large proportion of their output, as can be seen from the figures below. Their major markets are North America, other parts of Europe and the Afro-Asian countries. In the case of the United Kingdom which exports 40 per cent of all vehicles produced, the largest single customers are the United States, Canada, South Africa, New Zealand and Australia.

The United States, on the other hand, exports only about 3 per cent of its output, but due to the magnitude of this there is quite a sizeable export trade.

TABLE 6. *Principal vehicle manufacturers 1964 and 1968*

	PRODUCTION (in millions)	
	1964	1968
UNITED STATES	9·0	10·7
WEST GERMANY	2·9	3·1
UNITED KINGDOM	2·3	2·2
JAPAN	1·7	4·1
FRANCE	1·6	2·0
ITALY	1·1	1·7

AIRCRAFT

The aircraft industry is one which in many ways resembles that of motor vehicles. Like the latter it is light and multi-component, but it is far more complex, and the market is, in most countries, limited to airlines and governments.

It is most highly developed in the United States, the Soviet Union, Great Britain and France. All these countries have the necessary industrial and technical base, and they have considerable need for the aircraft. On account of the vast size of the two super-powers, air travel is the most efficient means of passenger travel inside them. In the United States production is very widespread, and the east and west coasts are of the greatest importance.

The two European countries are by comparison very small, and have less developed internal air services. They need aircraft, however, for their worldwide networks of communication. Both capitals, London and Paris, make components, and in Britain, Coventry, Bristol and Gloucester are important centres.

FACTORS IN THE LOCATION OF INDUSTRY

It will be seen from this general survey that most branches of industry are interdependent, and develop or decline in closely related groups. Yet each industry has its own particular requirements which may be rather different from those of others. There are, however, a number of overall factors which help to explain the presence of industry in particular regions.

POWER SUPPLIES. Coal is the oldest, and still the most important, source of power for large-scale industry. Until quite recently it was extremely costly and difficult to transport, and so the industries of North America and Western Europe grouped themselves on or near to the coalfields. Throughout the present century this pull of the coal-fields has been decreasing because of a number of changes which have been occurring.

1. Improved transport facilities and economies in consumption have made it more economic to transport coal long distances.

2. Large quantities are now converted into thermal electricity and gas which can be made available over large areas by means of transmission and pipelines.

3. Other sources of power, in particular oil, natural gas and hydro-electricity are strong competitors with coal.

Because of the greater mobility of all sorts of fuel and power today, the effect of the newer sources of supply has been to move industry away from the coalfields, but not necessarily to locate it at any other particular power source. The different sources have attracted certain types of industry. For instance hydro-electricity favours aluminium smelting, and petroleum motor-vehicle manufacture (California). However, for most industries it is advantageous to have the power supplies at not too great a distance, otherwise the cost of transport will be uneconomic.

RAW MATERIALS. In most of the great manufacturing regions the supplies of raw materials became inadequate early on, and now large imports have to be made of such things as natural fibres, metals, oils and chemicals. Many of the most advanced manufacturing regions such as New England and the London Basin produce hardly any of the multitude of raw materials they are continuously fabricating. However, in recent times more and more new industries have been springing up at or near the sources of raw material. As we have already seen, textiles are a notable instance of this, and it has been possible by the greater mobility of power, enabling it to be taken to the raw materials rather than vice versa as was usual formerly.

LABOUR SUPPLY. The availability of labour of the right type varies very considerably from one part of the world to another. In some countries, such as Japan, the large population is a major industrial asset, while in such countries as Australia development is slowed down by the labour shortage.

The same sort of situation can exist within individual countries, so that there may be unemployment in one part and a surplus of jobs in another. Many of the older countries are finding that it takes a great deal of adjustment to get the jobs to the people or, alternatively, the people to the jobs.

The nature of the available labour is another thing which limits its usefulness. While India has an immense population, the greater part of it is quite unsuited by tradition or education for industrial activity, and training is necessary on a large scale before more complex manufactures can be produced. At the other end of the scale, in the advanced industrial regions the labour is skilled, but it is also more costly and inflexible. This is one reason for the decentralisation of industry in the USA from the north-east to the formerly underdeveloped south and west. Nevertheless, the existence of a trained labour force is one of the remaining advantages possessed by the older industrial regions.

MARKETS. It has been said that the best market for a country's industries is its own people. It is the home market which generally creates the demand for particular products, and so makes expansion and exporting possible. The largest markets for most, though not all, manufactured goods are those countries having high standards of living. The most important of these are the North Atlantic countries and their 'outliers' in other parts of the world. Within the North Atlantic industrial regions one of the most notable tendencies has been for industry to become more and more 'market orientated', that is to say, for industries to move away from power and raw materials towards the consumers. This can be seen in the rapid growth of the industries of the Middle Atlantic region of the United States, and of the London and Paris regions in Western Europe. These compensate for their lack of physical resources by their large and relatively affluent populations.

TRANSPORT FACILITIES. Good communications by road, rail and water are essential (Chapter 11). Each of these three will have their places in a well-balanced industrial region. Mountains can be barriers causing great difficulties of communication: the Rockies, for instance, isolated California and helped to slow down that state's development. Water transport is the cheapest and most efficient over long distances, especially for heavy goods. Thus coastal and estuarine sites or those on interior waterways are highly advantageous. The influence which has been exerted by sea communications can be seen from the fact that almost all the major industrial regions of the world are on or near coasts (Fig. 32).

Changes in the Location of Industry

With the growth of new industries during the present century and the decline of many of the older ones, great changes have taken place in the location of industry within the established industrial regions themselves. Great Britain herself, with her long industrial history, illustrates very well the nature of such changes.

CHANGES IN GREAT BRITAIN. British industries have three main types of location. There are those which are situated around the fringes of the highlands on or near to the coalfields; there are those situated in the lowlands, mostly in the south and south-east of the country, and finally there are those on the coasts.

1. Those near to the coalfields are mostly industries with a long history. They include iron and steel, shipbuilding, cutlery, textiles and chemicals. Many of them have declined as a result of increasing overseas competition coupled with a decrease in the demand for the product. This has resulted in considerable social and economic distress accompanied by large-scale contraction in production. However, within this overall picture, there are certain industries which have remained very prosperous, notably cutlery and pottery industries of Sheffield and Stoke-on-Trent respectively. In both cases the reputation of the manufacturers and the special skills needed have helped to bring about this result.

2. It is in the lowlands that most of the newer industries have settled. These areas, such as the London Basin, have little in the way of raw materials, and the establishment of industry here illustrates a major change in industrial location which has been taking place throughout the world. The main centres of the new industries are the London and Birmingham regions. Birmingham and its neighbouring 'Black Country' were of considerable industrial importance previously, but they are even more so now. It used to be said that Birmingham made everything from a pin to a railway engine, but more characteristic today are motor vehicles together with their components, and electrical and domestic equipment. London has long been important for clothing and furniture, but to these are now joined the same type of miscellaneous manufactures as are found in the West Midlands. The growth of industries in these regions has been referred to as the 'drift to the South'.

3. A further development which is found around both highlands and lowlands alike is what we would call the 'drift to the coasts'. Deepwater bays and estuaries suitable for importing raw materials and for communications with other parts of the country are proving ideal for setting up a variety of industries like oil refining, chemicals and metallurgy. This development started a long time ago with the movement of industry to the coasts adjacent to the coalfields in South Wales

and the North-East. Now the Thames, Solent, Severn and Mersey are all expanding rapidly with industries based on heavy imports.

Such changes in the economic geography of Great Britain as have been outlined here can be regarded as the growing pains of industrial development, but they have unfortunately been accompanied by acute distress. As a result of this, since the late 1930s, it has been the policy of successive British governments to attempt to spread the most prosperous industries more widely by introducing them into regions which had suffered recession. A number of regions have been designated 'special development areas' and industrialists are encouraged to move into them. Some of the hardest-hit regions were South Wales, the North-East and central Scotland, and in all these areas a great deal has to be done to breathe fresh life into them and so help them join more fully in the general prosperity.

STUDENT WORK

1. Explain why the proportion of the world's shipping made in British shipyards decreased from 58 per cent in 1913 to 10 per cent in 1964.
2. What factors have contributed to the growth of chemical industries at (*a*) Tees-side, (*b*) Marseilles and (*c*) the western Ruhr?
3. On a map of the world, plot the production of synthetic rubber by means of proportional circles using the figures given below.

	Output in metric tons
USA	1,608,453
CANADA	178,701
UNITED KINGDOM	125,318
WEST GERMANY	106,471
FRANCE	96,944
ITALY	94,500
JAPAN	89,545
NETHERLANDS	85,000

Describe the distribution of production, and explain the factors which underlie it.

4. What factors have encouraged the concentration of textile production in New England? Assess the extent to which these factors are operative at the present day.

5. In what ways are the following industrial locations advantageous at the present day?
   (*a*) The linen industry in Northern Ireland.
   (*b*) The silk industry in Lyons.
   (*c*) The cotton industry in Catalonia.

6. With the aid of a sketch map, explain the main factors which have been responsible for the concentration of the American motor-vehicle industry in the Detroit region.

7. Study the figures for motor-vehicle production in 1968 on p. 132, and compare them with those given below for 1957.

UNITED STATES	7,220,520
WEST GERMANY	1,212,232
UNITED KINGDOM	1,149,000
FRANCE	927,956
ITALY	351,799
JAPAN	134,856

   (*a*) From these figures, work out the percentage change in each country between 1957 and 1968.
   (*b*) Comment on the nature of the changes which have taken place.

8. Write an account of the industries of Scandinavia, showing how they are related to the resources of the region.

9. While the industries of the north of Belgium are expanding rapidly, those of the south are on the decline. Attempt to explain this 'drift to the North' in the light of the geographical background.

10. Write an account of the Sheffield cutlery industry, explaining the inertia which it has displayed.

11. Compare and contrast the characteristic industries of the Midlands with those of central Scotland, and explain the differences you find.

12. The first British factory of the Ford Motor corporation was at Trafford Park, Manchester, and this was later moved to Dagenham. In 1958 a new plant was opened on Merseyside. Explain fully the geographical background to each of these moves.

13. What reasons can you give to explain the fact that California has now the fastest expanding industries in the United States?

Chapter 8
World Food Supplies

THE supply of food to the world's industrial populations has now become a highly specialised activity, involving a worldwide trading system. While the presence of supplies of raw materials has been a direct cause of the growth of the great centres of industry, by contrast the location of food production has been the result of the existence of those centres. Although at a primitive level the capacity of a region to provide food will determine the numbers of its people, to provide for the needs of more advanced societies foodstuffs are brought long distances from all parts of the world. Thus food production today is of two sorts:

1. SUBSISTENCE. This is producing foodstuffs for consumption by the growers. Such a system is now rare in the advanced countries, although quite common in less developed ones, but even in the latter there are likely to be exportable surpluses of crops used mainly for subsistence; and even in highly commercial agriculture, the farmer will probably produce many things for his own needs.

2. COMMERCIAL. This is specialised agriculture where the greater part of the produce is to be sold. Coffee in Brazil, wheat in Canada and cattle in Argentina are examples of such specialisation, in each case using the favourable local conditions to produce competitively.

WORLD TRADE

From the trade point of view there are two kinds of foodstuffs. There are those such as fresh milk, vegetables and soft fruit which, because of their cheapness and perishable nature, are produced as near as possible to the markets, and, secondly, there are those such as cereals, meat, coffee and tea, which can be stored easily and transported long distances. Only rarely are commodities of the first type transported any distance, and they are often produced near to the consumers, even when natural conditions are not ideal. In recent years, however, the distinction between the two types has become blurred by the increasing use of refrigeration and fast transport, which enable perishable goods to be produced at greater distances from markets.

Until the last century, long-distance trade in foodstuffs was confined for the most part to luxuries which could be afforded only by the well-to-do. As trade in such things grew, so prices became lower, till eventually they became virtually essential in the major countries. In so doing they often replaced local produce. In Great Britain, for instance, honey gradually gave place to sugar, beer and cider to tea, and tropical spices became more used than local herbs.

Until the middle of the nineteenth century the staple foods in Western Europe were obtained in sufficient quantities from local agriculture. Then the population began to outstrip food supplies, and at the same time new inventions like the steam-ship and, a little later, refrigeration made it possible to bring in temperate foods from North America and the Southern Hemisphere.

It will therefore be seen that the pattern of world trade and production has evolved basically in order to make up the deficiency of foodstuffs in Europe and to add to them exotic produce which would not otherwise have been available. However, in recent times the dominant position of Europe has been decreasing, and other regions, notably South-East Asia and the Americas, have become large food importers. The significance of present changes will be more fully realised as we go on to study the individual commodities. These will be considered under the headings of tropical produce, cereals, pastoral foods and finally fruit and vegetables.

TROPICAL PRODUCE

Tropical produce entering into world trade derives either from plantations (see p. 23) or from smallholdings. The method employed will depend on the agricultural and social structure of the particular area, and many important crops are grown on both. The most important of these crops are cane sugar, tea, coffee, cacao, fruits, culinary oils and spices. Of these, fruit is dealt with on p. 162, and oils are considered together with all the vegetable oils in Chapter 3.

CANE SUGAR. The sugar cane is a tall tropical grass from which sugar is extracted. This is then crystallised to make various sorts of solid sugar, treacle and molasses. The plant has no distinct harvesting season, but it needs to grow for between one and two years before it is ready for cutting. The best conditions for growth are when temperatures are over 21° C. (70° F.) and annual rainfall over 1,250 mm (50 inches),

Fig. 41. Tropical Foodstuffs: America

falling so as to provide a constant supply of water. Maximum yields occur when the soils are well drained and fertile.

Between them Latin America and South-East Asia account for about three-quarters of the world's total supplies. The tropical maritime regions of Central America, the West Indies and eastern Brazil have good climatic conditions, and they also have long-standing trading relations with the large markets in North America and Europe. The largest producers in the area are Brazil and Cuba with annual productions of 77 million and 40 million tons respectively in 1967, and there are also large outputs from Argentina and Ecuador. Since the breaking off in 1962 of trade relations with Cuba, its largest supplier, the United States has had to look elsewhere for supplies, and the Cubans for new markets. Most of the home supplies of the Americans come from the Gulf States, and in recent years production here has been increasing rapidly. Hawaii and Puerto Rico, respectively a state and a possession of the United States, also make a considerable contribution to the country's supplies.

The largest Asian producers are India and Pakistan, which between them grow a quarter of world output. The middle Ganges and Punjab are the centres of production, and in the latter area irrigation is used. Egypt's large crop has also to be grown with the aid of irrigation by the Nile waters. In recent years Australian output has been increasing rapidly and is now the largest outside the Americas and South-East Asia.

TEA. This evergreen bush is believed to have originated in China, and to have spread from there into other parts of South-East Asia. Tea drinking is now widespread not only in this region but also throughout the world. The development of large-scale production on plantations has been closely related to the demand for tea in Europe, and especially in Great Britain.

The tea bush produces a perennial crop, and it can only be grown successfully where frost is almost non-existent. Conditions have to be warm and humid, with a minimum rainfall of 1,000 mm (approximately 40 inches) falling so as to provide continuous water throughout the main growing period. Well-drained, rich and slightly acid soils are a further requirement.

TABLE 7. *Tea production in the four major producing countries, the USSR and Malawi*

(figures in 1,000 metric tons)

	1953	1962	1968
INDIA	279	344	403
CEYLON	156	212	225
CHINA	85	154	159 (1967)
JAPAN	40	78	85
USSR	20	37	58 (1967)
MALAWI	6	14	16
WORLD TOTAL	595	1,030	1,027

These physical conditions prevail in hilly parts of South-East Asia, and the countries of this region account for 90 per cent of world production. The largest producers are India, Ceylon, China, Japan and Indonesia. India alone grows 32 per cent of the world total, this coming mainly from Assam in the north-east, and the Nilgiri Hills in the south. The plant is cultivated on terraces designed to catch both the sun and the heavy monsoon rainfall, and at the same time ensure adequate drainage. Most of the crop is from large estates, many of which are owned by Europeans, and these benefit from the large local supplies of labour. The leaves are picked a number of times in one season, and these 'flushes', as they are called, are then dried in humidified huts before being exported. The close trading relations between India and Britain within the framework of the British Empire also encouraged the growing of this crop. About 60 per cent of India's tea harvest is normally exported, and of this 80 per cent goes to Britain.

Both China and Japan have been growing tea for far longer than their southern neighbours, and their home consumption is far greater. The tea, which is 'green', that is to say dried in the direct rays of the sun, does not enter much into world trade, Japan's exports making up only 10 per cent of her output.

The Soviet Union is a large tea consumer, and her home production has been increasing considerably of late. This is entirely confined to the extreme south of the country, and particularly the Caucasus.

COFFEE. This is another tropical bush, the physical requirements of which are very similar to those of tea. It must be free from frost throughout the year, have high temperatures for growing and sun for ripening the berries. A rainfall of 1,000 mm (around 40 inches) is sufficient, but best results are usually obtained where it is much heavier. Rich, well-drained soils are essential.

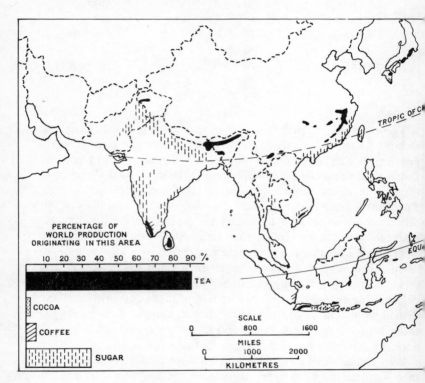

Fig. 42. Tropical Foodstuffs: South-East Asia

Nevertheless, the producing regions of coffee are entirely different from those of tea. Production is highly concentrated in the countries of Latin America, which account for over a half of the world's supplies. Brazil alone with nearly 1½ million tons per annum is responsible for a half of these, and the other most significant producers include Colombia, Mexico, Guatemala and Salvador.

Coffee-growing in Brazil centres on the south-east of the country, and particularly the state of São Paulo, where the estates stretch well into the interior. A number of local advantages present here include the sea mists of late summer which prevent the beans ripening too soon, the sunny autumn for picking and drying, and the rich 'terra roxa' soils, ideal for this exhausting crop. Production is on large estates known as 'fazendas', and these employ a large labour force to tend and pick the crop. The area is near to the coast, a fact which aids transport to the exporting ports of Santos and Rio de Janeiro. The principal customer for Brazilian coffee is the United States, which buys nearly a half of all that enters into world trade. Considerable quantities are also sold to Europe from Brazil and other Latin American countries.

The remainder of world production comes from South-East Asia and central Africa. The African countries are increasing their output of this and other plantation crops, and larger quantities from these sources are entering into world trade. They now account for over one million tons per annum, the largest producers being Ivory Coast, Angola, Uganda and Ethiopia.

CACAO. Besides being used as a beverage (cocoa), the beans of the cacao tree are also used in making chocolate and confectionery. The tree needs hot, moist, equable conditions, with temperatures above 27° C. (80° F.) and a minimum rainfall of 1,000 mm (40 inches) falling so as to provide a constant water supply. The greatest producing region is West Africa, which accounts for 70 per cent of the world total (Fig. 43). Output is concentrated in the south and slightly inland from the poorly drained coastlands, and the largest producers are Ghana and Nigeria. It is grown on smallholdings and makes an important contribution to exports. Brazil is the third world producer, and here it is grown on large estates on the eastern coastlands.

SPICES. Spices are a small but important constituent of diet, being used to add flavour to many types of foods. The most important are pepper, cloves, ginger, cinnamon and nutmeg, and the main producing regions are the West Indies, West Africa and South-East Asia. The West Indies produce large quantities of ginger and nutmeg, while Malaya and Indonesia, the 'Spice Islands', both produce pepper, nutmeg and cinnamon. The world's main source of cloves is the tiny island of Zanzibar off the coast of East Africa.

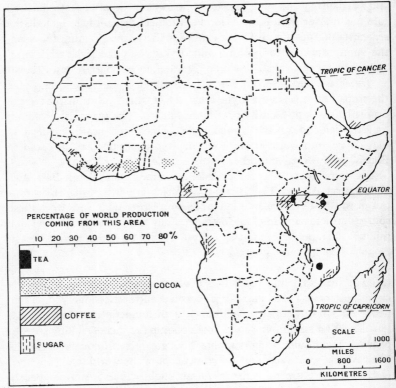

Fig. 43. Tropical Foodstuffs: Africa

CEREALS

These are members of the grass family, and their starch-producing grains are a basic diet for most of the world's people. Each of the half-dozen or so most important ones flourish in different physical conditions.

Wheat

This is the most important cereal used for human consumption. A native of the Middle East, it is grown over a wide range of latitude from the tropics to 55° North. The minimum growing season is three months, and the best rainfall range is 380 to 630 mm (approximately 15 to 25 inches), with plenty falling in the growing period. Low atmospheric humidity is preferable, with dry sunny weather for ripening and harvesting. The two main varieties are winter and spring wheat. The former is planted in the autumn, and this is only possible when the winters are not too severe. Spring wheat is planted in areas like Canada, the USSR and northern USA which have long cold winters.

The best soil for wheat is a clayey loam, retentive yet with good drainage. Particularly excellent is the rich black soil known as 'chernozem', which develops under a vegetation of temperate grassland.

Such conditions are best found towards the centres of the mid-latitude continents. Europe (including the USSR) and North America between them account for 65 per cent of the world's crop, the USSR with 80 million tons per annum being the world's largest producer (Fig. 44). The wheat area here centres on the 'black earth' belt in the south of European Russia, but cultivation has spread eastwards into the 'Virgin Lands' of Soviet Central Asia. These stretch latitudinally between the cold lands to the north, and the dry ones to the south, finally petering out in the mountains of central Siberia. Although these regions account for the bulk of the country's wheat, in other parts the crop is integrated into the mixed agriculture. Collective farming is universal, and the land is worked in common by the peasants, who share the profits among themselves and provide the state with a quota of the produce. In size these farms can vary from hundreds to thousands of acres.

In spite of the large home production, the USSR has been forced to import wheat, and in recent years it has bought large quantities from Canada and the USA. This situation is only one aspect of the difficulties which have long been facing Soviet agriculture, and to which the following factors have contributed. (1) Setbacks in the Virgin Lands settlement: since the Second World War the boundaries of cultivation have been pushed eastwards, and many problems, such as drought and removal of the topsoil, have been encountered. (2) Bad harvests have occurred during a number of recent years, often due to the unreliability of the rainfall. (3) There has been a shortage of fertilisers to combat soil exhaustion. (4) The rigid centralised control of agriculture which was characteristic of the Soviet Union until recent years discouraged initiative in either workers or management.

In North America the wheat regions lie mainly between 90° and 100° West, where the physical conditions are similar to those of the

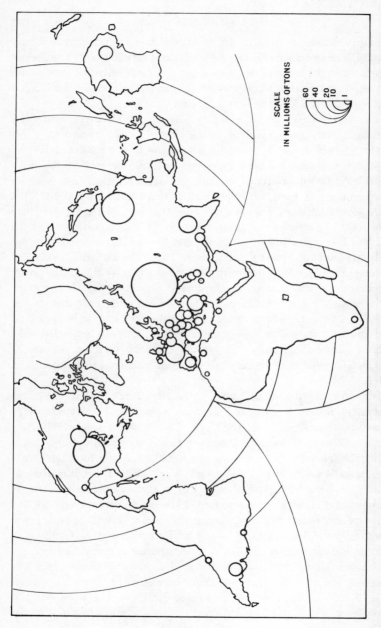

Fig. 44. World Wheat Production by Country

SCALE
IN MILLIONS OF TONS

60
40
20
10
1

USSR. Farm size varies generally from 140 to 200 hectares (350 to 500 acres) and the land is divided up into rectangular units with roads and railways following their boundary lines. The farming is highly mechanised, and closely related to the provision of transport.

This extensive producing region grew up to supply the industrial populations first of Europe and then of the United States. With its far smaller population, Canada exports a larger proportion of its crop – in a recent year 85 per cent as compared to 45 per cent from the United States. The main customer is Western Europe, and Canada has benefited from its close association with Great Britain, formerly as colony and today as a member of the Commonwealth. Furthermore, the Great Lakes provide a waterway almost as far in as the wheat 'Triangle', and since 1958 the new St Lawrence Seaway has opened the Lakes to ocean-going vessels, adding further to the ease of transport.

The countries of Western Europe are all important producers, and here the land is more intensively worked and yields are higher than those in other regions (Table 8). The largest outputs are those of France,

TABLE 8. *Wheat production in the six principal producers and the United Kingdom 1968*

(output in million metric tons; yields in 100 kilos per hectare)

	PRO-DUCTION	EXPORTS	IMPORTS	YIELDS PER HECTARE
USSR	93·4	5·8	2·1	13·9
USA	42·9	18·8	—	19·2
INDIA	16·5	—	6·4	11·0
FRANCE	15·0	2·9	0·6	36·6
ITALY	9·6	0·8	0·9	22·4
CANADA	17·7	10·3	—	14·9
UNITED KINGDOM	3·9	0·2	4·0	35·5

West Germany and Italy, although yields in these countries are lower than those of Great Britain, the Netherlands and Denmark. Western Europe also imports 14 million tons representing 35 per cent of all wheat entering into world trade. The main sources of imports are

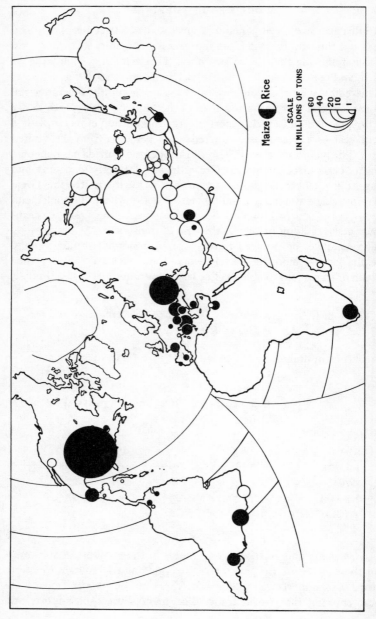

Fig. 45. World Production of Maize and Rice by Country

North America and the Southern Continents. Some European countries export sizeable quantities, mostly to their neighbours (Fig. 46).

Between 1953 and 1962 the world production of wheat increased by 16 per cent, and between 1962 and 1968 there was a further increase of the same percentage, but this was spread very unevenly. Countries which have traditionally been exporters showed either a decrease or no change, while the large consuming countries showed increases. This is illustrated by the decline of Canada's production between 1953 and 1962 from 17·2 to 7·7 million tons, followed by an increase to 18·7 million tons in 1968. The USSR, on the other hand, increased its production by 100 per cent between 1953 and 1968 (41 million to 80 million tons) and India by 45 per cent. At the same time imports into the Far Eastern countries rose from 3·5 million to 12 million tons. It is notable, however, that Canada has now begun to raise its output once more, partly no doubt in response to increased purchases by Communist countries.

Maize

Maize or Indian Corn is a native of Central America, but it is now grown widely in warm temperate and tropical countries throughout the world. As a result of its climatic requirements, it is mostly grown equatorwards of the wheat regions. The growing season needs to be at least five months in length, with temperatures averaging over 21° C. (70° F.) for over three of these. The minimum rainfall requirement is about 635 mm (25 inches), falling so as to provide ample moisture through the growing period. Yields are best when the soils are deep and retentive.

The distribution of maize cultivation is more highly concentrated than is that of wheat, the most important growers being the United States, the Soviet Union, Brazil, Argentina, South Africa and the countries of southern Europe. By far the largest output is that of the United States, which accounts for nearly a half of the world total.

In the USA production is widespread through the eastern parts of the country, but the greatest concentration is in the 'Corn Belt' south of the Great Lakes. Here maize is king, and rarely is less than half the cropped land given over to it. Although the corn is used widely for human consumption, its bulk and high food value make it unrivalled as animal fodder. Cattle raised on the Great Plains to the west are brought eastwards for fattening, and large numbers of pigs are reared on it (see p. 159). This system of farming is geared to supply the large urban populations living at a high standard and consequently eating more meat than cereals. Thus three times as much corn as wheat is grown in the United States. Between 1953 and 1962 corn output increased by 23 per cent, while over the same period that of wheat increased by only 6 per cent. Between 1962 and 1968 there was a further increase of maize output by some 14 per cent bringing it up to 110 million tons.

The rise in production of the Soviet Union has been even more rapid, and between 1953 and 1962 it increased from 5·8 million to 24 million tons. Very little of this vast country is really suited to the crop, and the main producing areas are confined to the southern and European parts. During the late 1960s the output of grain maize declined considerably due largely to the difficulties of producing it over much of the country, and to the increased emphasis on animal farming so that more maize is being cut green as fodder.

In Southern Europe it is the east which is the main maize producer,

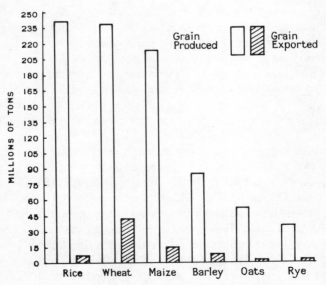

Fig. 46. World Production and Exports of Six Major Cereals

especially the Danube lowlands. Production in Western Europe is increasing, and the combined output of the Common Market countries, now standing at over 8 million tons per annum, makes up the greater part of it. France and Italy are by far the most important West European producers. Northern Argentina, southern Brazil, Mexico and South Africa all grow large quantities, and in parts of these countries and in many others where standards of living are lower, it is an important basic item of diet.

World trade in maize, totalling 27 million tons, is only one-half that of wheat (Fig. 46). Nearly 50 per cent of it is exported by the USA, and 70 per cent of the imports are taken by Western Europe, mostly for animal fodder. In a wider sense, however, maize can be said to enter into trade in the form of the animals which it feeds.

Rice

With an annual production of over 275 million tons, this is produced in larger quantities than any other cereal (Fig. 46), and it is the staple diet of about a third of the world's people. Since it spends the greater part of its growing period partially submerged, large quantities of water together with a surface able to retain it are essential requirements. Besides this, a frost-free period of five months is vital, with temperatures in the main growing period of over 19° C. (56° F.). The highest yields come from regions with alluvial soils and high sunshine rates.

About three-quarters of the world's rice comes from South-East Asia. The largest producers are China, India, Pakistan, Japan and Indonesia. The most intensive growing regions are the great river valleys, together with their deltas and adjacent coastlands. Here the combination of flat alluvial land, high temperatures and monsoon rains make ideal conditions for growth. In such areas the rice is essentially a subsistence crop, and the high yields allow it to support huge populations, unfortunately mainly at low nutritional standards.

Rice can also be grown in regions where certain of the optimum conditions are lacking. In the absence of flat land, hillsides in South-East Asia are terraced, a method which is very common in Indonesia and Japan. If the rainfall is not sufficient, irrigation can be used. The oldest example of this is Egypt, where the natural flooding of the

Nile provides water and enriches the topsoil with its silt. The cultivation of rice with the aid of irrigation is now increasing in northern Italy, southern France, Spain and California, in all of which the hot sunny summers provide good ripening conditions.

World trade in rice accounts for only about 7 million tons per annum, or $2\frac{1}{2}$ per cent of production, and the greatest part of this trade is among the Asian countries themselves. The largest surpluses are in Thailand, which exports 20 per cent of its crop, and also Burma, Cambodia and South Vietnam. These countries have been called the 'rice bowl of Asia', and among them they export $4\frac{1}{2}$ million tons, mostly to Indonesia, Malaysia, Ceylon, China and India.

Other Cereals

Other important cereals are barley, oats, rye, millets and sorghums.

BARLEY does best in conditions similar to those favourable to wheat, although it is able to ripen in a shorter growing season. About a third of world production comes from Europe, by far the most important producer being the USSR. It is a major crop in most countries of the north and centre of the continent, where Great Britain and France are responsible for the greater part of the output. North America produces a further 13 per cent, and this is grown mostly in the wheat areas. The Middle East, Mediterranean lands, north China and India all grow considerable quantities. In most places this cereal is of little importance as a direct constituent of human diet, its main uses being as animal fodder and for brewing beer. Only about 6 per cent of the world's barley enters into trade, and the largest importers are the West European countries. In recent years the imports of barley for cattle fattening have been on the increase.

OATS thrive well where conditions are cool and moist, and need a longer growing season than does barley. The main growing areas are North America, Europe and the USSR, which together account for 85 per cent of the world's output. Only small quantities enter into world trade, and again the Western European countries are the main importers.

RYE is used widely for human consumption in those areas where it is produced. About 90 per cent of the total comes from Eastern Europe and the USSR and two-thirds of this from the USSR alone. This cereal is grown on the poorer soils of the North European Plain which are unsuitable for wheat.

MILLETS and SORGHUMS are native to warmer lands. The former is distributed widely throughout the Far East and parts of Africa, and is used as a human foodstuff. It can tolerate a considerable rainfall range, and in India it is cultivated alongside wheat in the dry north and rice on the humid coasts. It is, however, most typical of the dry poorer lands of the central Deccan. Sorghums are also grown as a food grain in the same regions, but the largest national production is that of the United States. There it is grown widely in the South and is used mainly for animal fodder.

POTATOES

These vegetables are being treated together with cereals because they have occupied a similar place in the diet of many countries. For instance, in Ireland during the last century, the population became excessively dependent on them for their staple diet, and when the crop failed there were widespread famines.

In 1967 world production was 300 million tons, and of this 210 millions came from Europe and the USSR alone. The USSR is the world's largest producer, accounting for 30 per cent of the entire crop, and other important countries are Poland and the two Germanys. Potatoes grow best where there is a long, cool growing season with low humidity, and are tolerant of poor sandy soils. This makes them ideal for temperate lands which are not suitable for wheat. They are grown in conjunction with rye, and their distribution is very close to that of the latter.

In addition to being a basic food crop, potatoes are also grown as a market gardening vegetable, particularly in Western Europe and North America.

PASTORAL FARMING

Pastoral or animal farming is, in one form or another, widespread throughout the world. The most important animals reared are cattle, pigs, sheep and poultry, although others such as goats and horses are of significance in certain areas. Pastoralism is, however, most developed in the temperate lands of both hemispheres. The main reasons for this are: (*a*) These are the best climates for the animals and their produce; in warmer regions such things as meat and milk deteriorate rapidly. (*b*) Crops like cereals, roots and grass, which grow well in temperate climates are the most satisfactory fodder for the animals. (*c*) Pastoral produce has always been an important part of the diet of the people living in temperate lands, and as these are now among the most populous in the world, the demand for the foodstuffs is naturally very great.

Cattle

With about 1,000 million head distributed throughout the world, these are the most important farm animals. They are most highly concentrated in Europe, North America, South America and India. In India for religious reasons, they do not contribute much to the food supply.

In North America the cattle are widely spread south of the Canadian Shield and east of the Rockies. The greatest concentration is in the Mid-West with its plentiful supplies of fodder and the great demand for beef and pastoral produce. While the Corn Belt concentrates on fattening, the cooler areas to the north of it are devoted to pastoral farming for the production of butter, milk and cheese. Farther west on the Great Plains stretching southwards from Canada to Texas, cattle ranching is dominant. The huge spaces and natural grassland favour rearing, and there is a shuttle service to the fattening regions farther east. In America's South the contraction of cotton cultivation and the increased demand for animal produce is encouraging the development of pastoral farming, and it is being helped by the introduction of cross-breeds and the use of new insecticides.

The greatest densities of cattle in Europe are found in the west, where the climate produces good pasture land, and the mild winters allow the cattle to feed out for much of the year. The best pasture land, especially near urban areas, is given over to dairying, while beef cattle are commonly fattened in arable regions. The Soviet Union is second only to the USA in the total number of its animals, and these are widely spread throughout the European part of the country where mixed grain and pastoral farming is the rule.

In the southern continents, much of the intensive cattle farming has been undertaken with an eye on the European food markets. The Campos of Brazil is becoming increasingly important, but the most intensive cattle country is the Pampas of Uruguay and north-east Argentina. Nearness to the coasts, flat land and the natural grasslands have combined to make this one large factory for producing beef. Comparable parts of Australia and New Zealand also have large numbers of cattle, but they are more famous for their pastoral produce.

WORLD TRADE. Beef is the most important of all meat entering into world trade. The largest importers are the European countries, which among them took 73 per cent of the 1·6 million metric tons which entered into world trade in 1968. The major importers are the United Kingdom, France, West Germany and the Benelux countries (Fig. 47). The principal exporters are Argentina, Australia, New Zealand and Uruguay. In recent years, as the populations of the exporting countries have increased, the surplus available for export has decreased. In Argentina this has been accompanied by considerable industrialisation which has absorbed many former agricultural workers. This, and similar developments in other producing countries goes far to explaining the world beef shortage of 1964.

At the same time the importing countries of Western Europe have been increasing their own productions, and many of them, notably France, are now exporters.

Fresh milk and cream are most ideally produced as near as possible to the consumers, but butter and cheese can easily be transported long distances. Again the Western European countries are the largest customers, among them importing 470,000 tons of butter. The United Kingdom is the largest single buyer, accounting on the average for 70 per cent of all imports. The largest exporters are New Zealand, Denmark, Australia and the Netherlands. The pattern of trade in cheese is a very similar one, although it takes in more countries. The United Kingdom, West Germany and Italy all buy large quantities, and the main exporters are the same as those of butter. There is also a growing trade among the European countries themselves.

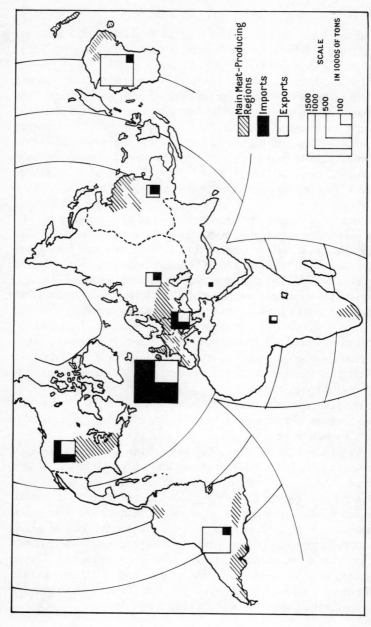

Fig. 47. World Trade in Fresh Meat and the Main Areas of its Production. Trade is shown by geographical regions and the boundaries of these are indicated by broken lines

Pigs

The world's 600 million pigs are far more highly concentrated into limited areas than are cattle. No less than 45 per cent of them are found in the USSR, Europe and North America (as compared with 24 per cent of the world's cattle). Their distribution is related very closely to the other features of the agriculture, and often owes more to economic than to physical factors. They can be very well integrated into a mixed farming economy, converting surplus crops and waste products into pork and bacon.

In the United States, the Corn Belt is the centre of pig rearing to an even greater extent than it is of cattle, and for similar reasons. Farther south, pigs can be kept on smallholdings more profitably and flexibly than can cattle. In Europe the animals are widespread, and are of especial importance in Denmark, north Germany and parts of Eastern Europe. Denmark is an intensive producer of bacon, which is exported to many other European countries, particularly Great Britain.

Another part of the world which has large numbers of pigs is central China, especially the Red Basin of the upper Yangtse valley.

Poultry

Like pigs these are fed off arable surpluses and also off waste products. Poultry farming is usually found near to large towns, or in suitable areas where good transport is available.

Sheep

Sheep reared for mutton and lamb are usually different breeds from those which are good wool-bearers. The meat animals prefer milder conditions and heavier rainfall to the others but there are now many multi-purpose crossbreeds. Both Great Britain and New Zealand are noted for the quality of their meat, and the former country imports large quantities from the latter. Britain is the world's largest consumer, and New Zealand's production has been developed with the British market in mind. More and more animals are now being slaughtered young for lamb, especially for the markets of those countries whose standards of living are able to support this rather expensive way of obtaining the meat.

THE FISHING INDUSTRY

Fish are the only important natural product which now make up a part of human diet, although fish 'farming' of one sort or another is increasing in importance.

Most of the water areas of the globe contain fish, but they are not exploited for foodstuffs in all of them. The most important fishing grounds are the temperate seas of the northern hemisphere, particularly off the western coasts of Europe, the eastern coasts of Asia and the eastern and western seaboards of North America.

Western Europe

The main fishing grounds here are the North Sea, the waters encircling the British Isles, and the coastal waters off France, Norway and Iceland. These areas yield such fish as cod, mackerel, herring, sole and plaice, and the largest catches are landed at ports in Great Britain, West Germany, Norway and France. The main advantages of this region for fishing include: (1) The richness of the seas in edible fish. This is due to the large quantities of plankton and other fish food being brought coastwards by such currents as the North Atlantic Drift. The shallow waters of the Continental Shelf are breeding grounds for the fish, and certain exceptionally shallow places such as the Dogger Bank are famous for their immense catches. (2) Fishing is made much easier by the excellent port facilities afforded by the deeply indented sunken coastlines. Most fishing-boats are still quite small, and the bays and estuaries provide them with much-needed harbours. (3) The large markets of the great industrial regions are rarely far from the coasts and are linked to the fishing ports by fast transport (Fig. 48).

Shellfish, like lobster, crab and oysters, are found in large numbers in the shallow waters around the coasts, and their numbers are kept up by spawning areas which are particularly suitable. Similar techniques are used to keep up the numbers of river fish, the most important of these being trout and salmon.

Other Regions

Along the eastern coasts of North America are the important fishing grounds of Newfoundland (Grand Banks), the Gulf of St Lawrence

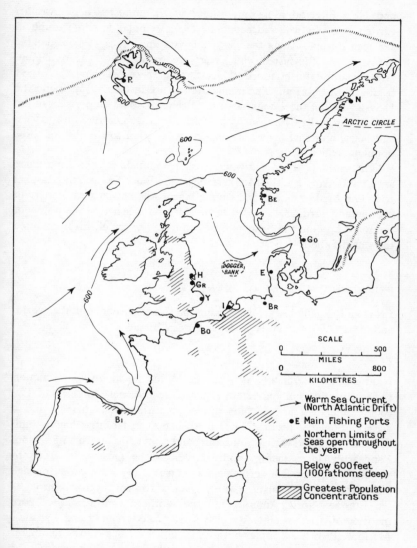

Fig. 48. The Fishing Industry of Western Europe. *Main ports:* Be – Bergen,
Bi – Bilbao, Bo – Boulogne, Br – Bremen, E – Esbjerg, Go – Gotenburg,
Gr – Grimsby, H – Hull, I – Ijmuiden, N – Narvik, Y – Yarmouth, R –
Reykjavik

and New England. The importance of the industry here owes its existence to physical and economic factors similar to those found in Western Europe. Along the western coasts there is also a considerable industry, and the fast-flowing rivers are particularly rich in salmon. In terms of total fish landed, the eastern coasts of Asia have the largest fishing industry of all. The main landings are in China, Japan and the U S S R, each of these countries accounting for about 10 per cent of the world's catch. In China and Japan fish farming is carried on in rivers and lakes, and this makes an important addition to the diet of these populous regions.

Other parts of the world where commercial fishing is of importance are Central America, the Mediterranean, the Black Sea and the Caspian Sea. The Mediterranean and similar warm seas have a great variety of fish, notably sardine, tuna and carp. Sturgeon is fished in the waters of the Black Sea and the Caspian Sea, and from the roe of this is obtained the world-famous delicacy, caviar.

FRUIT AND MARKET GARDENING

Fruit and vegetables are important foodstuffs throughout the world, and in parts of the wet tropics they replace cereals as the staple diet.

Fruit

Fruit is grown in most parts of the world, but for intensive production the warm and cool temperate regions are the most important. The cool temperate fruits include apples, plums, pears, cherries and a variety of smaller berries. They flourish best in localities having high sunshine rates and with low humidity and rainfall in the growing season. Land with slopes facing south or west is the most satisfactory, to provide protection from growing season frosts, to secure good drainage and to trap as much sun as possible. Fruit of this sort is grown throughout Europe, North America and the southern continents. In more maritime districts such as western England, Normandy and Canada's Maritime Provinces, apples both for eating and cider are the dominant fruit, as they are more resistant than others to high humidity and cloud cover.

The most uniformly excellent regions for fruit production are, however, those having Mediterranean climates (Appendix 1). The main reasons for this are the exceptionally high sunshine rates, low humidity in the growing season, and the autumn and winter rainfall dominance. In the European Mediterranean the steep slopes together with well-

TABLE 9. *Mean sunshine hours for selected stations*

	YEARLY TOTAL	MONTH WITH MAXIMUM
OXFORD	1,473	193 (May)
BERLIN	1,614	247 (June)
ROME	2,362	348 (July)
ATHENS	2,655	364 (July)

drained and often lime-rich soils are further advantages, and similar conditions are to be found in the other Mediterranean regions. The most characteristic fruits in these areas are grapes, peaches, apricots, olives, oranges and lemons, together with certain cool temperate fruits.

PRODUCING REGIONS. In the European Mediterranean area it is the western part, the Tyrrhenian Basin, which has the most specialised production. It benefits from having better natural water supplies and from its nearness to and close connections with the large markets of North-West Europe. Important specialisations are grapes (southern France, northern Italy and Algeria), olives (Italy and Spain) and citrus fruits (Spain and Italy). Cultivation of the vine is by no means confined to Mediterranean regions, but is practised very considerably throughout many European countries. The plant likes very good drainage, light soils and is commonly grown on terraced slopes. Western Europe alone accounts for 65 per cent of world wine production (see Table 10).

In the eastern parts of the Mediterranean important developments are occurring, particularly in Israel, which is using large-scale irrigation to bring formerly arid land into production.

California is to North America what the Mediterranean is to Europe, but it has the great problem of vast distances from the great eastern consuming centres. This problem is surmounted by canning and processing the produce and this enables the world to be its market. Furthermore, the population of the west coast is increasing rapidly, and this enhances the importance of the local agriculture.

TABLE 10. *Wine production: world and selected countries*

(figures in 1,000 hectolitres)

	Average 1960–62	Average 1966–68
FRANCE	60,267	63,167
ITALY	59,130	69,212
SPAIN	19,670	26,977
USA	10,400	12,817
USSR	7,650	15,750
WORLD TOTAL	240,000	281,650

Fruit and wine are also produced in large quantities in the similar regions of Australia, South Africa and Chile. Like the other commercial food producers south of the Equator, these have northern markets very much in mind. In the USSR wine output has increased in recent years, particularly that of the Caucasus and Transcaucasia where physical conditions are very suitable. The cultivation of fruit is characteristic of the southern part of European Russia where deciduous fruit orchards are widespread. The citrus and other fruit production of western Siberia has also been increasing with the aid of large-scale irrigation projects.

In the intertropical regions the commercial production of fruit has been handicapped by the fact that most of it does not travel well. Two fruits of considerable significance are bananas, grown in the West Indies, Central and South America and parts of Africa; and pineapples, particularly characteristic of South-East Asia.

Trade in fruit is limited by its perishability, and therefore proximity to consumers and fast transport are advantages which have acted in favour of producers within manageable distances of the great markets. Those which travel best are citrus fruits, pineapples, bananas and apples, and so long as moderate care is taken, they can be transported long distances under modern conditions. Britain, for instance, receives apples from Canada, and a great variety of fruits from Australia and South Africa. Those regions from which the transport of fresh fruit is very difficult, or which have unmarketable surpluses, have always attempted to preserve or process their produce in some way, and export it in that form. California and the southern continents all produce wine, tinned fruit, dried fruit, oil and juice which can be readily transported, and for which there is a large demand in Western Europe and the United States. In Europe the making of wine is an old-established industry and the largest output comes from France and Italy; Spain and Portugal are famous for their sherry and port. Europe's internal trade in fresh fruit is considerable, particularly between the southern producing and the northern consuming centres.

Market Gardening

The intensive production of vegetables and flowers, known as market gardening, is most highly developed in Western Europe and North America. These vegetables include potatoes, peas, beans, carrots, onions, lettuce and many others, and they thrive best when conditions are cool and moist, and soils are deep and retentive. A long growing season is an advantage, as this enables supplies to be kept up for a longer period. Economically it is also advantageous for them to be grown as near as possible to the markets to reduce transport costs.

In Western Europe regions which are particularly suited physically are the western Netherlands together with other parts of the composite delta of the Rhine, and the English Fenlands. They have well-balanced alluvial soils, flat land and good water supplies. Market gardens also cluster round the great cities, such as Paris, London and Brussels for economic reasons (Plate VIII). There are also two other types of location: (1) Those areas, such as Cornwall, Brittany and the Channel Islands, where mild winters have encouraged the growing of early fruit and vegetables. (2) Areas where the hot summers are suitable for growing tomatoes, melons and other vegetables which do not normally grow well in North-Western Europe. Important producing regions for these are alluvial parts of the Mediterranean lands, such as the lower Rhône and the coasts of eastern Spain.

At present a revolution is occurring in the marketing of vegetables which is invalidating traditional ideas, and will probably have radical effects on the distribution of production in the future. It is increasingly becoming possible for vegetables to be transported longer distances, and to be put on the markets as required. This is because (a) bulk freezing and improved canning methods enable 'fresh' produce to be made available out of season; (b) faster communications by road, rail and air enables growing to concentrate in the most suitable areas, even if these are far from markets; (c) specialisation has been encouraged by greater trade among the European countries themselves and the breaking down of old trading barriers.

In the United States a high degree of specialisation has already occurred, and there is an immense 'truck-farming' area stretching down the eastern seaboard southwards from New York. Vegetables are also grown in large quantities in California where ideal conditions are provided by the alluvial soils of the Central Valley and the irrigation water.

A root crop which is very different economically from the vegetables we have been considering is sugar beet. This is now making a substantial contribution to the world's sugar supplies, and total world production is now 160 million tons. This crop requires physical conditions approximating closely to those favoured by wheat, and the two are now very closely associated. The largest output comes from the USSR, which accounts for nearly a half of the world total; other large producers are the USA, France and West Germany. After crushing to extract the sugar, the waste can be used as animal fodder.

THE FOOD SUPPLIES OF WESTERN EUROPE

It will be clear from the foregoing that Western Europe is the largest importer of foodstuffs, and has had more influence on the pattern of world trade in them than any other region. Yet this area is also itself one of the most important food producers, and is rapidly becoming even more so. The agricultural economy varies from the specialised and highly mechanised agriculture of the Netherlands and Denmark, to the near subsistence peasant farming still common in parts of Spain and southern Italy. Considered according to produce, the three main categories of farming in the region are cash crop, pastoral and intensive.

1. The main area of cash-crop farming is located in a great belt stretching eastwards from northern France, through Belgium and into north Germany. The major crops here are cereals, especially wheat, barley and sugar beet. In this area the climate is drier than farther west,

and there is more sunshine and higher growing season temperatures. The soils are for the most part deep and well-drained, and over a large area a loess soil has developed on the underlying chalk and limestone. The flat or slightly undulating land is ideal terrain for large-scale and mechanised farming. A similar agricultural system is to be found in eastern England and parts of the Po valley; the latter is the most important rice-growing region in Europe.

2. Pastoral farming is of greatest importance in the lowlands of central and western England and France, in the North European Plain from the Low Countries to Denmark and in parts of the Alps. The mild moist lowlands of western Britain and France are unrivalled for the quality of their grass and fodder crops, and this has made them famous for their milk, butter and cheese. Farther east in the Netherlands, Denmark and north Germany, cattle and pigs are fattened on grains, roots and skim milk. Many Alpine and sub-Alpine districts are important for their dairy produce, and cattle transhume from the upland pastures where they spend the summers, to winter in the lowlands.

Two other animals are of importance in certain regions only. The greatest concentrations of sheep are in the marginal lands of western Britain and central Spain, and those of goats in the Mediterranean uplands. As food producers sheep are kept for their meat, and goats principally for milk and cheese.

3. Specialised farming for fruit, and vegetables, as we have already seen (p. 165), is confined to those limited regions which are particularly suitable. In general the main areas of fruit production are found in the south and east, and those of vegetables in the north and west.

IMPORTS AND EXPORTS

Western Europe is both the largest importer and the largest exporter of foodstuffs in the world. However, the imports, worth approximately £7,000 million per annum, are over twice the value of the exports. A great deal of the foreign trade of these countries, and especially the exports, is with their neighbours. In the case of the six Common Market countries, 23 per cent of their imports and 43 per cent of their exports are accounted for by trade within the group. The United Kingdom is responsible for a quarter of all Western Europe's food imports, and is the world's largest single importer. As we have seen, she draws her supplies from all parts of the world, but her trade with other European countries has been increasing rapidly in recent years.

Although on balance the region is a food importer, three countries –

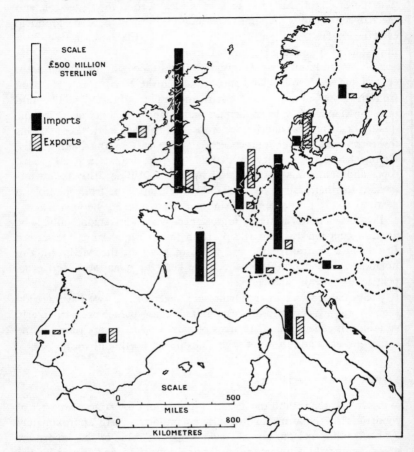

Fig. 49. Western Europe. Value of Imports and Exports of Foodstuffs by Country. Black bars represent imports and shaded bars represent exports

the Netherlands, Denmark and Ireland – have a surplus of exports over imports (Fig. 49). The Netherlands and Denmark, with their intensive production of pastoral produce and meat, export a great deal to their neighbours. France and Italy also export large quantities particularly cereals, fruit and wine.

WORLD TRADE

Although Western Europe is so pivotal to world trade in food, it by no means monopolises it. The countries of North America come next in the value of their food trade, and exports exceed imports by about one-quarter. The exports are in the main surpluses of temperate grains, meat and fruit, and the largest group of imports is that from tropical countries (Fig. 50). Australia and New Zealand export six times as much food as they import, and the bulk of their exports are of temperate foods to Europe, and especially Great Britain. The food imports of the Asian and African countries are on a much smaller scale, and mostly consist of basic foodstuffs. A great part of South-East Asia's imports are from other Asian countries (p. 153), but there is an increasing trade with Australia and North America. The USSR does not figure largely in the world's food trade, except for imports of tropical produce and, more recently, of food grains.

Differences in the nature of the imports will be clearly seen by reference to Fig. 50. Food imports into the United Kingdom in 1968 were valued at £1,711 millions. Of these the three main groups were meat 23 per cent, fruit and vegetables 20 per cent and cereals 13 per cent. By contrast India's imports only totalled one-sixth those of the United Kingdom, and 95 per cent of them were cereals, mostly rice and wheat. Similar features are seen in the imports of Japan, 40 per cent of which were food grains. The United States is now second only to the United Kingdom in the value of its food imports. No less than a half of them are tropical products, which are among the few things in which this rich country is deficient.

It will be appreciated from this brief survey of world food production and trade that there is an immense variety in both commodities and methods of production. A substantial part of the world's agriculture is engaged in producing foodstuffs which may be destined to supply populations living great distances away, while the rest is producing to supply only the wants of the immediate locality. The type of production which is found in any area will depend on its physical suitability to particular crops, the amount of food surplus available and the general economic

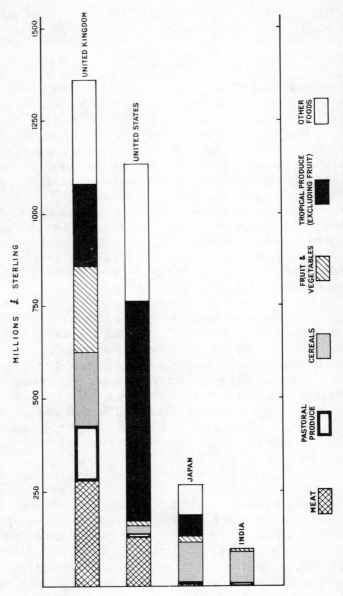

Fig. 50. The Composition of the Food Imports of Certain Countries

level. The food industry is now undergoing radical changes as a result of the raising of standards of living, the removal of trade barriers and the development of new techniques in production, transport and storage. The present trends can be summed up under three headings:

1. The countries of Europe are increasing their own output of food-stuffs and at the same time trading more with one another. This means greater self-sufficiency on a continental level and a decrease in the imports of many commodities. In the United Kingdom, for instance, gross national output of food between 1953 and 1963 increased by 30 per cent and by 1968 home production was providing for over 50 per cent of needs (by value).

2. Larger quantities of imports are being taken up by other regions, notably North America and South-East Asia, the former to add variety to its diet, and the latter to help overcome the long-standing mal-nutrition of its peoples. At the same time the great Asian consuming countries have been rapidly increasing their own food output.

3. The industrialisation of the temperate food exporters is taking more and more people off the land, and increasing the home demand for foodstuffs. At the same time many of their traditional markets have become more unstable, and new markets are being canvassed. This issue was brought out into the open during the debate on Britain's admission into the Common Market in 1962, when adverse repercussions on the country's major suppliers were envisaged.

STUDENT WORK

1. Why is there a far greater production of tropical plantation crops in the countries of South-East Asia than in those of Central Africa?
2. What do you consider to be the main reasons for the differences in the world distributions of production of tea and coffee?
3. Using the figures on p. 143, draw bar graphs to show the production of tea in the principal producers in 1953 and 1968. Comment on the information revealed by these graphs.
4. Compare and contrast the systems of farming found in the Corn Belt of the United States and in the Ganges Valley of India. Show what part physical and economic factors have played in creating the differences between them.

5. Study the following production figures for maize:

	Production (in million tons)
USSR	18·3
USA	96·1
FRANCE	2·4
ITALY	3·7
CANADA	0·8

Compare these with the figures for wheat production on p. 149, and account for the differences in the output of the two grains in the countries concerned.

6. Write a comparative account of the production of dairy produce in the USA and the USSR, explaining the influence exerted by the natural and economic backgrounds in each case.

7. Write an essay on the production of fruit in either North America or Africa, explaining the main factors influencing production in the continent chosen.

8. What advantages for a fishing industry are possessed by the eastern seaboard of North America?

9. Consider carefully the information given below on land utilisation in the United Kingdom and Japan:

	Total area (square km)	Arable and orchard (%)	Permanent pasture (%)	Forest (%)
UNITED KINGDOM	244,000	30·4	49·4	6·3
JAPAN	369,700	13·7	1·8	67·7

Attempt to explain the differences which these figures show, and assess their implications for the food supplies of the two countries.

10. Write an account of the main features of the agriculture of France.

11. The following are the percentages of the land under arable and orchard in three European countries:

IRELAND	18·6%
DENMARK	62·9%
SWITZERLAND	11·8%

Describe briefly the nature of the arable land in each case, and account for the differences among them.

12. Write short notes on the following:

Collective farming; Tropical plantation agriculture; Subsistence farming; Ranching; Market gardening.

13. Using Table 10, describe the main features of world wine production, and comment on the changes which have taken place between 1960–62 and 1966–68.

Chapter 9
Population

THE world's population in 1964 was reckoned at some 3,250 millions, and by 1969 it had grown to 3,552 millions, an increase of nearly 10 per cent. This is distributed very irregularly over the earth's surface and while vast areas have scarcely a single inhabitant, others have thousands to every square mile. Parts of the hot deserts have proved so uninviting to man that they have remained almost empty spaces, while by contrast in Europe there is not enough space to go round and people are packed horizontally and vertically into great cities.

The population of any area is both the cause and the result of its economic possibilities. It is a cause because in the economic sense 'manpower' is a resource just as much as coal or iron. It is, in fact, one of the most important of all resources, since there are substitutes for the others, but not, as yet, for human beings. The manpower must be adequate to economic needs, and if it is not, then it must be made up by natural increase or by immigration. Hence it comes about that the density of population is an index of the success of a particular area in providing a living, since the richer the area the larger the numbers who can be supported.

The population of any area can be regarded as being both labour supply and consumers. In primitive communities with little trade and a subsistence agriculture, the same people will both produce and consume the goods. As the economy evolves the community will range more widely for its supplies, and trade will produce specialisation. Some degree of specialisation is the normal thing in the world today, and a Malayan rubber planter would no more consider using all he produced, than would an operator on a Coventry assembly line.

Ideally the population should be the number who can be adequately supported by the economy. Unfortunately it is common to find that a population is not being adequately supported, and the result can be either general poverty or a high rate of unemployment. Such a situation can be caused either by a steep rise in population, so outpacing its resources, or by a decline in productivity.

There are a number of factors which may be responsible for the density of population in any area:

AGRICULTURE. An intensive agriculture with high yields per acre will normally be able to support more people than an extensive one with low yields. Where the land is given over to market gardening, as in south-west Holland, the small size of holdings together with the large labour requirements encourages a high rural population density. On the other hand, in upland Wales with its large sheep farms, the labour requirements are small and the area is thinly populated. Even in intensive farming, greater efficiency and mechanisation will lower the labour requirement. In the American Cotton Belt, for instance, the mechanisation of picking has contributed to the drift away from the land.

INDUSTRY. By comparison with agriculture, industrial activity is highly concentrated, and the industrial populations will also be concentrated. They are mostly town-dwellers, and the densities are among the highest in the world. Although some industry is carried on in most countries, its relative importance, as we have already seen, varies very considerably. In Great Britain 95 per cent of the population are non-agricultural, while in India this section makes up only 30 per cent.

COMMERCE. Trade encourages population growth at ports and route towns. In London and New York commercial activities of one sort and another occupy a large section of the population. In places such as Singapore and Colombo, whose intermediate location on sea routes has made them convenient entrepôts, the proportion is even larger.

RESIDENCE. The bulk of people have to live where there is work to be found, but during this century an increasing number have been endeavouring to work, and even more to retire, where they find it pleasant to live. This is usually because of the climate and the nature of the scenery, and such places as the Mediterranean coasts have become deservedly popular. The attraction of large cities, especially capitals, is great, not only economically, but for social and cultural reasons as well. These things go far to accounting for the fact that such metropoli usually have a disproportionately large share of a nation's population.

POLITICAL. Capital cities, especially those built for the purpose, are the most obvious examples of population concentrated for political reasons. The activities of Washington, Canberra, Ottawa and Brasilia, to name but a few, are completely bound up with those of their respective governments. Political decisions also influence population distribution in a more general way. The desire of the Soviet government to locate as much of its industry as possible well away from the western frontiers has been an important reason for the large increase of the population east of the Urals. Between 1939 and 1961 this increased by 30 per cent while during the same period the nation's total population increased by 9·5 per cent. Another political decision was the expulsion of 14 million Germans from that country's former eastern territories after 1945, so swelling the population of West Germany with refugees.

THE DISTRIBUTION OF THE WORLD'S POPULATION

Broadly speaking, it will be convenient to group the world's population into areas where it is high, where it is moderate and where it is light.

The three regions which contain the most populous areas are South-East Asia, peninsular Europe and east-central North America. Together these regions have about two-thirds of the population of the world's land area.

By far the greatest populations are found in South-East Asia, which with 1,800 million contains nearly a half the world total. In this area are China with 730 millions, India with 524 millions, Indonesia with 115 millions, Pakistan and Japan with 110 and 100 millions respectively. The greatest concentrations are to be found in the plains and valleys drained by the rivers Hwang Ho, Yangste, Si Kiang, Red and Ganges. The bulk of the people here are dependent on the prolific agriculture, but the fact that so many can be supported keeps living standards to a minimum. High populations are also found around the coasts, and on adjacent islands like the Japanese group, Taiwan (Formosa), Luzon and Java. Here industry and commerce have played a big part, and many of the people live in large ports, notably Tokyo, Shanghai and Singapore.

The second largest concentration is that of peninsular Europe with 430 million inhabitants, 220 million of whom live in the four most populous countries: Great Britain, France, West Germany and Italy. The highest densities are to be found in the industrial countries, with Great Britain averaging 227 per square kilometre, and the Netherlands 380. Even these figures mask the much higher ones which are found only in urban areas, and rural populations make up a relatively small proportion of the national totals.

The third, and smallest, region is east-central North America, with about 100 million people. Its structure is very similar to that of Western Europe, and we shall be considering it in more detail later on.

In addition to these three, there are a number of other areas of high population density in various parts of the world. The most significant are West Africa, Egypt and parts of Central America. In each it is the intensiveness of the agriculture which is the prime cause.

At the other end of the scale are the lightly populated regions, with below ten inhabitants per square kilometre. These generally uninviting places include the deserts, where the rainfall is as a rule quite insufficient to support much agriculture. Then there are the very cold regions around the poles, and the very hot regions around the Equator, which, for opposite reasons, have proved unsuitable to much human occupation. Finally there are the high mountains which, due to a variety of disabilities, have remained thinly populated.

Between these two extremes are the areas of moderate population, such as are found in parts of the Middle East, Africa south of the Sahara, and the southern USSR. These and similar areas have large rural populations with patches of urban development.

It can be seen from this that extreme conditions of one sort or another have discouraged intensive human settlement. On the other hand the areas of temperate or variable climates have high, or at least moderate, populations. Two contrasting examples of populous regions are the Indian subcontinent and Anglo-America.

The Indian Subcontinent

This region includes that part of Asia south of the Himalayas and enclosed by their outliers. It includes the countries of India, Pakistan, Ceylon and Burma. The combined area of these four is 5 million square kilometres and in 1968 their total population was 670 millions. This is about one-fifth that of the world on one-twenty-fifth of its land area. The overall density is 119 per square kilometre, but there is immense variation. In the Himalayas and the Thar desert there are large un-populated stretches, while West Bengal and Kerala have average densities per square kilometre of 395 and 433 respectively.

As in other parts of South-East Asia the greatest concentrations of people are found in the river valleys and coastal lowlands. In this case, the valley and delta of the Ganges–Brahmaputra have the largest numbers. Here conditions are especially favourable to intensive agri-culture based on rice cultivation, and rural densities of over 750 people per square kilometre are common. The relationship of population density to rice cultivation is very close, and when rice is replaced by other cereals, such as wheat or millet, the numbers supported are invariably far lower.

The subcontinent's rate of population increase is above the world average of 1·7 per cent per annum. In India it is 2·2 per cent, and in Pakistan 2·1 per cent. This is still not as great as in many other countries where there is nothing like the population problem: Australia has a current increase of 2·3 per cent. What makes it alarming is the large existing population. Between 1951 and 1961 the population of India proper increased by 21·5 per cent which was 75 million people. Between 1962 and 1968 there was a further increase of 19 per cent which was now 84 million people. Over the ten years from 1951 North America's population increased by 22 per cent, but in this case the increase was only 37 millions (Fig. 51).

This continued increase is one of the main internal problems facing the countries of the subcontinent, and especially India itself, which is burdened with three-quarters of it. As in other countries, the basic cause of the increase is the steady decline in the death-rate, consequent on improved hygiene and medical attention. Infant mortality alone has been halved in the last twenty-five years. The largest growth is in the big cities, into which there is a steady influx of people from the countryside. The subcontinent now has eleven millionaire cities, having a total population of 26 millions. This is an increase of 128 per cent since 1951, when these same cities had 11·4 millions. Great distress results,

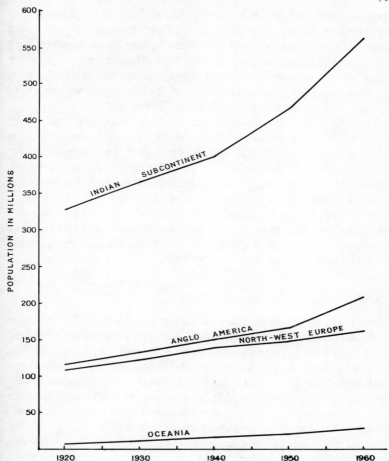

Fig. 51. Comparative Population Increases. (North-West Europe includes the United Kingdom, France, Belgium, Netherlands, Luxemburg, West Germany and Denmark)

since work does not become available as rapidly as the number of town-dwellers increase.

The resulting problem of overpopulation is being tackled in many ways. An attempt is being made to slow down the birth-rate, but this is a long-term business, and little can be expected in the short term.

Irrigation and reclamation schemes, such as those in the Indus valley and the Punjab, aim to take pressure off populous areas by resettling some of the people in new lands. Productivity is being increased through improvements in agricultural efficiency, and many large estates are being broken up so as to turn over the land to the peasants. Moreover, the steadily growing industrialisation of the country is the spearhead for an attack on low standards of living (Chapter 10).

It is not large populations which are a problem, but rather large populations living in areas which cannot at present support them adequately. The average population density of West Bengal is very similar to that of Lancashire, but the living conditions of the people are totally different. Such is the magnitude of the task that India has to move forward as fast as she can in order to stay in the same place. The growth in numbers is swallowing up both foreign aid and increases in production. The task of stabilising the population and raising living standards is one which is likely to be occupying this part of the world for some time to come.

Anglo-America

This area of 19·4 million square kilometres comprises the United States and Canada, and its population in 1968 was 222 millions. This is just one-third that of the Indian subcontinent on three and a half times its area, and it produces an overall density of twelve per square kilometre. Although Canada is slightly the larger country, its population of 20·7 millions is only one-tenth that of the area as a whole. This gives Canada a density of two per square kilometre, while that of the United States is twenty. However, the greater part of Canada's population lives in the south of the country near to the United States frontier, while much of the Canadian Shield and the Rockies is almost empty.

Ninety per cent of the people of the United States live east of 100° West, the very marked boundary between the moderate and low densities being the point at which rainfall becomes insufficient for agriculture. The greatest concentration lies between the Great Lakes and the Atlantic coast, covering almost the same area as that of the Manufacturing Belt (see Chapter 7). It contains twelve of the thirty-two millionaire cities in Anglo-America, and twenty-six of the sixty-eight cities of over half a million people. The American states included in this area have a combined population of 85 millions, which is 42 per cent that of the United States as a whole on 8 per cent of its surface. Densities are very high, New York State having an average of 136 per square kilometre, and New Jersey of 333.

Such concentration is comparable to that found in South-East Asia, but the causes are entirely different. Here intensive industry and trade are responsible rather than intensive agriculture. In fact, the north-eastern part has rather poor agricultural development. The Manufacturing Belt itself is not continuous, but is a collection of large commercial and industrial cities, and this is reflected in the grouping of the population in clusters. In between there is much agricultural land on which the densities are far lower. In recent years, however, increases of population have been more rapid in other parts of the country, one notable such area being California. The five millionaire cities of this state now have a combined population of 13 millions and the total population is over 20 million, one-quarter that of the Manufacturing Belt and one-tenth of the total United States population.

This is a very different picture from India with its consistently high level of rural population, stretching for thousands of square kilometres over the rich flat land.

The rate of population increase in North America as a whole is lower than that of the Indian subcontinent, although that of Canada (2·1 per cent) is as high as that of India. This is accounted for both by natural increase and by the continued high level of immigration. After the tremendous immigration into the United States which took place in the nineteenth and early twentieth centuries, it has now been severely restricted on a quota system. With the slowing down of the economic growth rate, the need for large increases in the labour supply has diminished. Indeed, mechanisation and automation are making large numbers of workers redundant. Due to changes in the nature and location of industry there are patches of high unemployment, and the main problem is one of co-ordinating available labour and industry in the same place at the same time.

We have been considering two populous areas which in all other respects are in complete contrast to one another. The one has among the world's highest total populations, and available land is used intensively for agricultural purposes. The other has a smaller population, the bulk of which is clustered into a few dozen large urban and industrial centres. The former has among the lowest and the latter the highest standards of living in the world.

Although every part of the world is unique in having its own special population structure and problems, these two examples in many ways typify other areas. India bears close resemblances to the other monsoonal lands of South-East Asia, while North America has much in common with the other great industrial areas, mostly found in temperate latitudes.

STUDENT WORK

1. Describe briefly the main features of the distribution of population in North-West Europe. Assess the importance of the various factors which have influenced it.
2. The following population figures refer to three republics in the USSR:

	Area (1,000 sq. miles)	Population (in millions)
UKRAINE	232	41·8
UZBEKISTAN	158	8·1
TURKMENISTAN	188	1·5

Describe briefly the geographical background to these areas, and explain the differences shown in the population.
3. Why have Canada's North-West Territories got a population density of below one per square kilometre, while that of Ontario averages five per square kilometre?
4. Compare and contrast the distribution of population in Nigeria and Egypt relating it in each case to the physical and economic background.
5. Attempt to explain the rapid growth in India's urban population since the end of the Second World War.

Chapter 10

Problems of the Developing Countries

THE problems of economic development are worldwide, and are as real in rural Wales as they are in Pakistan. Yet in certain countries, like Pakistan, they are more in evidence because these countries are poor, and are having an uphill struggle to improve their standards of living. They are referred to as the 'underdeveloped' or, more appropriately, the 'developing' countries. It is difficult to define them exactly, but they are generally considered as being most of the countries of Latin America, Africa and Southern Asia. They form a great bloc situated astride the Equator, and mainly, although by no means all, within the tropics. A good indication of those countries which consider themselves as coming within this category is given by those which attended the United Nations Conference on Trade and Development (UNCTAD) in 1964 (Fig. 52). To these must be added similar countries which did not attend, either for political reasons or because they were still dependent territories. The group, the 'Geneva 77', contains nations at varying stages of development, but they have in common the fact that they all depend heavily on exports of primary produce, and they all aim to manufacture more for themselves.

The countries making up this great slice of the globe contain 70 per cent of the world's people, but have only 12 per cent of its energy consumption. The value of its manufactured goods is only 7 per cent of the world's total. There are, however, great differences between one region and another. Brazil's energy output is sixteen times that of the countries of East Africa combined (Table 11). Africa and the Middle East combined are only responsible for one per cent of the world's manufactures and 2 per cent of its energy consumption. Latin America consumes two and a half times as much energy as Africa.

The reasons for this backwardness are varied, and can rarely if ever be put down to a single cause. The climate and environment have

TABLE II. *Area, population and energy production of selected countries*

	AREA (1,000 sq. km)	POPULATION (millions)	ENERGY PRODUCTION (million tons coal equivalent)	ENERGY PER CAPITA (kilos)
EAST AFRICA (Kenya, Uganda, Tanzania)	1,756	29·8	0·15	84
BRAZIL	8,512	85·7	15·9	392
INDIA	3,268	511·1	79	176
UNITED KINGDOM	244	55·1	179·6	5,003

over a long period proved unfavourable to progress and it is only a wide range of modern equipment and techniques which is enabling natural difficulties to be surmounted. Almost all these countries are former European possessions (Fig. 1) and the Afro-Asian countries have only gained their independence since the Second World War. Moreover, the role of these areas as furnishers of raw materials to the countries of the Northern Hemisphere has discouraged their own industrial growth. The most important of the problems which these countries face are low standards of living, malnutrition, disease and widespread lack of education. Many of these factors have a bearing on agriculture.

AGRICULTURE

Agricultural problems will naturally differ from one region to another, but in the developing lands there are certain ones which are common to most of them.

1. Throughout most of the humid tropics the soils are poorer in plant foods than are those of temperate latitudes. This is because of the rapidity with which organic matter and minerals are leached away, and soil erosion in areas of heavy rainfall. These, as well as unscientific methods of cropping and grazing, are important causes of low yields.

2. Pests and diseases present formidable obstacles in all tropical lands. In particular, yellow fever and malaria, carried by mosquitoes, lead to inertia; and in Africa large tracts of land are rendered unsuitable

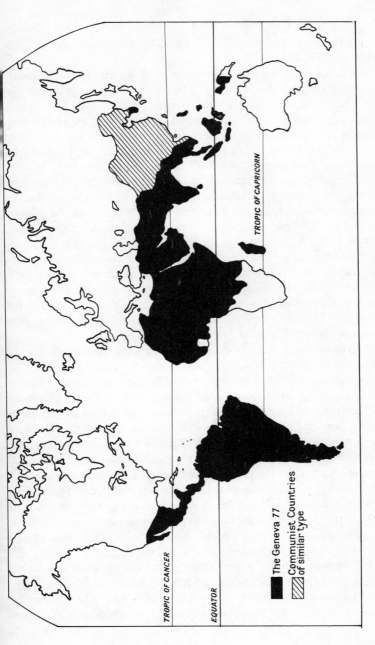

EQUATOR

TROPIC OF CANCER

TROPIC OF CAPRICORN

■ The Geneva 77

▨ Communist Countries of similar type

Fig. 52. The Developing Countries

for cattle by the many species of tsetse fly which transmit sleeping sickness and nagana.

3. The agriculture is often insufficient both in quantity and in quality to provide adequate food supplies. The strong bias towards cereals and vegetables causes the diet of the people to be deficient in animal proteins and fats, calcium and vitamins. Rice is an example of a crop which is able to support large numbers of people but at low nutritional standards, and it is in the rice-growing lands that the problem of food deficiency is most acute.

4. Unreliability of the harvests due to inadequate rainfall, insect pests or some other cause. In subsistence agriculture such unreliability can be quite disastrous, and in the past has caused great famines over large areas.

5. Local social and agricultural systems can slow down the pace of change. In India, for instance, the smallness of the holdings has made it difficult for the peasant to earn a living out of the land, and this has encouraged him to accumulate huge hereditary debts. At the same time, there are great difficulties involved in persuading peasants to accept new ideas. There are also religious taboos such as the sacredness of the cow to the Hindus which means that what would otherwise be large resources are totally unused.

6. Excessive specialisation in one or more commodities is a feature of plantation agriculture which ultimately acts to its disadvantage. By depriving the economy of other sources of income, it can have effects as bad as the specialisation in coal production in South Wales and Durham did earlier this century. The growers of, let us say, rubber in Malaya, or sisal in Tanzania, to quote two examples, sell the bulk of their produce outside their respective countries, and therefore are dependent for their revenue on the world demand. If and when there are changes in this demand which make the price fall, the consequences will inevitably be serious. An example of excessive concentration was that of Brazil upon coffee: the demand rose in the years before 1914; this was followed between the two world wars by a steep fall in demand, and Brazil was left with large surpluses which she could not sell. This caused acute distress to a large section of her agricultural population.

7. Transport. Wherever large-scale agriculture has been developed, such as that of the Canadian Prairies and the Argentine Pampas, corresponding transport facilities have been built up. The developing countries cover huge areas, and transport is essential before new

agriculture and industry can be successful. The reason for building most of the railways of West Africa, for instance, was to take certain commodities to the coast for export, and the region is still lacking in good internal lines of communication. There is everywhere need for more railways and roads, built to help economic growth.

These problems are being tackled in a variety of ways by those countries which face them. In many areas the land under cultivation is being extended, and people from overcrowded areas resettled on it. The Punjab is a notable example of a large area which is being irrigated by the waters of the great rivers which flow through it. Similar schemes have been undertaken in Egypt, Sudan, Ghana and other countries. Not only does irrigation bring new land into use, but it can improve the usefulness of existing agricultural land. Its function is to store water and to supply it when and where it is required, and this helps eliminate drought and floods, two of the major hazards. Added to this is the use of fertilisers and insecticides, and the introduction of new agricultural methods. The cacao tree in West Africa, for instance, has long been affected by the diseases of swollen shoot and black pod which progressively reduce output and finally kill the trees. These are now being combated by the policy of removing infected parts and applying insecticides. A problem which is almost as great is the prejudice of the local farmers who are reluctant to have new ways tried out.

In this field the work of European settlers should be noted. They came in large numbers to North, East and South Africa, but with the granting of independence, many have left or been forced to leave. They were pioneers in the introduction of new methods of farming, and in many areas their presence has been of great value.

Diversification of the agriculture is a more long-term affair. Brazil has learned a salutary lesson from her crises during the interwar period. In the last thirty years there has been a large increase in her production of cotton, citrus fruits, sugar and rice, and the agriculture is now more broadly based. In Africa similar developments are afoot. Nigeria, which earns a third of its foreign currency from palm oil (p. 42), has in the last decade been increasing its output of rubber, cocoa, cotton and animal produce. Naturally the best use must be made of a country's ability to grow for the market, but a wide range of products is both an insurance against slumps in demand, and an encouragement to the setting up of new home industries.

Pastoral Farming

It has already been seen that pastoral farming is not one of the strong points of tropical agriculture, and in very few places have animals been really successful. It is estimated that animal products supply only about 5 per cent of the calories of the people who live in these regions. Cattle are, of all animals, found in the largest numbers, but the great heat decreases their productivity, and encourages the diseases which are harmful to them. The natural savanna grassland makes poor fodder, having a low content in such things as phosphorus, and the dry seasons present the difficulty of finding enough water. In addition, meat, milk, butter and cheese do not keep well in hot countries, and good transport facilities are needed to market them.

In spite of these difficulties, cattle are found in many areas. On the Brazilian Campos, ranching is an occupation of long standing and has achieved considerable success. Over large parts of Africa also cattle are to be found, particularly in the drier areas of tropical continental climate where there is natural grassland and a certain degree of protection from disease (Fig. 53). The most common breeds include the humped zebu and dwarf shorthorn, but certain others are found within the tsetse-fly-infested regions and are resistant to it. Progress in this industry will depend upon the extent to which it proves practicable to immunise animals and to introduce new resistant varieties which at the same time have a good yield of meat and milk. Other necessities are the provision of adequate supplies of water by digging new wells and pumping water from other sources, and growing fodder crops suitable for the animals.

INDUSTRY

If one of Britain's problems is that her industries are old, one of those facing the developing countries is that of getting their industries started. Most of them have industrialisation as a top priority, and some among them, like India and Egypt, have already an impressive record of achievement behind them. Some of the problems of industrialisation are very similar to those of agriculture, but there are also a number of special requirements.

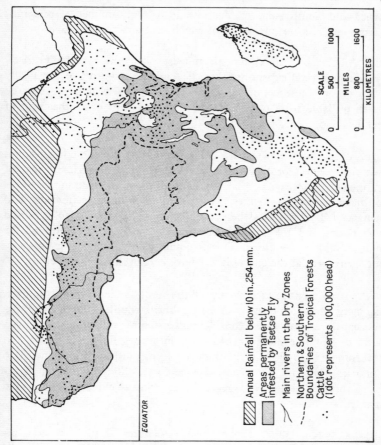

Fig. 53. Difficulties Facing Pastoral Farming in Africa South of the Sahara

POWER AND RAW MATERIALS. We have already seen that the output of power in most of these countries is low, and in most cases it is inadequate to support even a modest industrial structure. In the Middle East and Latin America there is a huge petroleum output, but most of it is exported. Very little is converted into power for the use of the producing country. It is power more than anything else which decides a nation's capacity to manufacture, and it is therefore a high priority for development. Many of these countries, particularly those of Central

Africa and South America, are rich in a large number of minerals, ferrous and non-ferrous, many of which are hardly touched.

AID. All forms of development, and especially the basic enterprises, need huge capital expenditure, far beyond the resources of practically every one of these countries. It is therefore vital that large sums be made available from other nations, either as loans or in the form of technical aid.

EDUCATION AND TRAINING. It has been said with some justification that the greatest problem facing the developing countries is that of ignorance. Education is vital for all sections of the community so as to make successful factory workers no less than technicians and managers. This requires the setting up of more schools, colleges and universities and the sending of students to the universities of the more developed countries. This is bound to be a long-term business, but the returns at the end of it will have been well worth the effort.

POLITICAL STABILITY. Many of the newly independent countries, like many of the old ones, have their political troubles, and the resulting internal unrest can cause considerable economic difficulties, and even put a brake on development. In addition to this, foreign investors and governments are likely to be deterred from putting their money into countries whose future may seem uncertain. Political stability is therefore a very real necessity to create the right sort of climate for economic growth.

COMPETITION. One of the great difficulties facing the new industrialists is the competition of goods from the established industrial countries. These can often be imported cheaper and better than local ones can be produced, stifling the local industries before they have got on their feet.

Industrial Development

Since the provision of power is obviously vital to industry, it is not surprising that power projects should be a built-in feature of the efforts of the developing nations to industrialise. The most impressive of these are the schemes for producing hydro-electric power, which at the same time provide irrigation water. In Africa the largest of these are the Aswan High Dam (opened in 1964) in Egypt, the Khashm el Girba and Roseires dams in Sudan, Kariba on the Zambesi and the Volta and Kainji projects in Ghana and Nigeria respectively. The power generated from these giants is intended for domestic and industrial use over wide areas.

In starting up industries successfully in new areas, there are also two other requirements. These are that the raw materials should be at hand, and that the actual operations of manufacturing should be relatively simple. These requirements have made textiles a popular starter in many fibre-producing areas. In India and Pakistan the spinning and weaving of cotton, silk and jute have long been carried out, and their products have proved highly competitive with those from Western Europe (Chapter 7). Other simple industries making use of local materials are vegetable oil pressing, clothing, shoes, fruit-juice extraction, brewing, milling, metal refining and the making of construction materials such as cement and bricks. Getting more favourable tariff arrangements for their goods is one of the main aims of the 'Geneva 77', and they have already achieved some success in this.

To accomplish this development foreign aid, in the forms of money, equipment and education, is vital. Only two countries in the world succeeded in industrialising themselves without foreign capital and these were the USSR and Great Britain, both very special cases. Loans, aid and capital investments have been going out from the industrial countries in a constant flow since the Second World War. Until a few years ago such aid was unplanned, and often savoured very much of Cold War manoeuvrings, but now there are a number of organisations through which the greater part of it is being channelled. In 1960 the late President Kennedy launched 'Alliance for Progress', an organisation designed to get the developed and prosperous parts of North and South America to help those parts which were underdeveloped and poor. In the same year the 'Economic Development Fund' of the Common Market countries came into operation. This is designed to provide aid to the associated members of the trade bloc in Africa, which were former colonies of France and Belgium. The greater part of Britain's aid goes to the Commonwealth countries, and the members of the 'Old Commonwealth' are now also providing aid and investment.

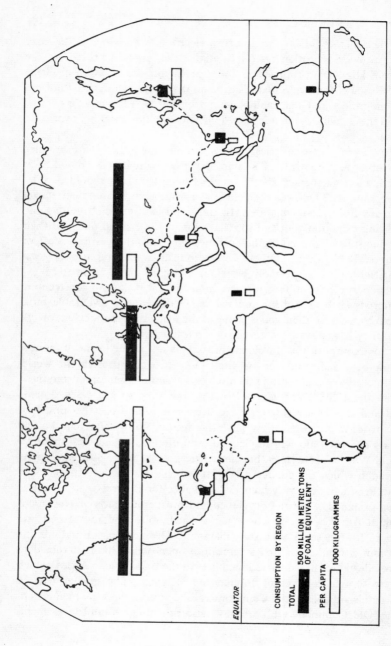

EQUATOR

CONSUMPTION BY REGION

TOTAL   ■ 500 MILLION METRIC TONS
           OF COAL EQUIVALENT

PER CAPITA □ 1000 KILOGRAMMES

Fig. 54. World Energy Consumption by Region. Boundaries of Regions are shown by dotted lines

In spite of the great achievement in international cooperation which all this represents, there is still a long way to go. In what we like to consider as being an age of progress, hundreds of millions of people are still living close to the 'bread line' as a result mainly of the difficult environments in which they live. This presents the world with one of its greatest problems, and it is in the interests of all, rich and poor alike, that it should be solved.

STUDENT WORK

1. Show in what ways agriculture has helped form a basis for industrial growth in the developing countries.
2. Study the following information concerning certain West African countries:

Country	Population (millions)	Area (1,000 sq. km)	Imports	Exports
			(million £ sterling)	
GHANA	6·7	239	140·8	104·4
NIGERIA	31·2	924	172·0	172·0
IVORY COAST	3·2	322	61·0	67·0
NIGER	2·8	1,267	5·6	5·9

Explain the differences revealed by these figures in the light of their geographical backgrounds.
3. Suppose a European company is going to build a modern integrated steelworks, and is considering sites in northern Algeria, Singapore and Venezuela. State what advantages and disadvantages would be found for the project in each case.
4. Discuss the problems which face the economic development of any one African country.
5. Write an essay on the production of food in India, considering the problems which are involved in providing sufficient foodstuffs for the population.
6. On an outline map, draw proportional circles to represent the total populations of each of the countries of either Latin America or South-East Asia. (Use the most recent information available to you.) Comment on the main features of the distribution, and relate it to the main features of the economy.
7. Write an essay on the problems of transport in either Brazil or the Congo. In what ways do these problems affect the development of the country chosen?

Chapter 11

World Communications
and Trade

IN order that products may be exchanged on a large scale over the surface of the earth, a very highly developed system of transport and communications is essential. During the past half-century, and to an even greater extent in the last twenty years, the world's means of communication have been revolutionised. In 1840 it took a fortnight to cross the Atlantic by ship, while today it can be done by air in a matter of hours. Similarly goods which in the last century took weeks in transit now only take days. This revolution has affected the efficiency of each of the main means of transport by land, sea and air. The particular method of transport which is chosen in any circumstances will depend upon the nature both of the goods and of the journey to be undertaken. In some cases, such as the movement of electricity, there is little choice, while in others, such as market garden produce, many different and often complementary methods are available. The one chosen will depend upon a number of things based on economic, social and even political considerations. In the light of these, here is an outline of the main methods of transport and their functions.

WATER TRANSPORT

Transport by sea is the principal method of exchanging goods between geographically separated regions. As a result of the needs of world trade and communications, a great web of sea routes now connects practically every part of the world. In its total traffic the most important route is that which links together the countries of Western Europe and those of North America. Another of great importance is the south Eurasian route connecting Western Europe with the Far East and Australasia via the Mediterranean, the Red Sea and the Indian Ocean.

This route was made possible by the opening of the Suez Canal in 1869, before which all sea traffic between Europe and Asia had to go around the Cape of Good Hope. Other routes of considerable significance are those between North and South America, and across the Pacific from North America to the Far East (Fig. 55). Communications between the western and eastern seaboards of the Americas and between the Atlantic and the Pacific focus on the Panama Canal completed in 1914.

In addition to these there are also numerous short-distance routes. Water transport is generally cheaper than that on land, although, of course, it is slower, and, by its nature, confined to more limited areas. It is particularly competitive for the transport of bulky goods which are of low value in proportion to their weight. A good example of this is the movement of petroleum by tanker from the Gulf States to the north-east of the USA, and the coastal traffic in coal from the Durham coalfield to London.

Since the mid-1960s there has been a considerable increase in the use of container ships. These make for more efficient transportation and for easier handling and dispatch of goods at the ports. There are now important container routes from Western Europe to North America, Australia and the Far East, and also across the Pacific from the United States to Japan and South-East Asia.

Closely linked to sea transport is the use of canals, rivers and other inland waterways. These can serve as extended arms of the sea stretching into the land, and also have their own independent systems of trade. Inland water communications have suffered much in the industrial countries from the competition of road and rail, but certain of them remain of considerable economic significance. In North America, the Great Lakes system carries large quantities of grain, coal, ferrous and non-ferrous metals, and wood, and links together the economies of the industrial regions around its shores. Many canals make up this great system of internal waterways, notably the Sault Ste. Marie (Soo) between Lakes Superior and Huron, and the Welland, which by-passes the Niagara Falls. The completion of the St Lawrence Seaway in 1958 opened up the heart of North America to ocean vessels which are now able to sail 3,500 kilometres into the continent. It has been aptly said that this has given Canada a southern coastline and the United States a northern one.

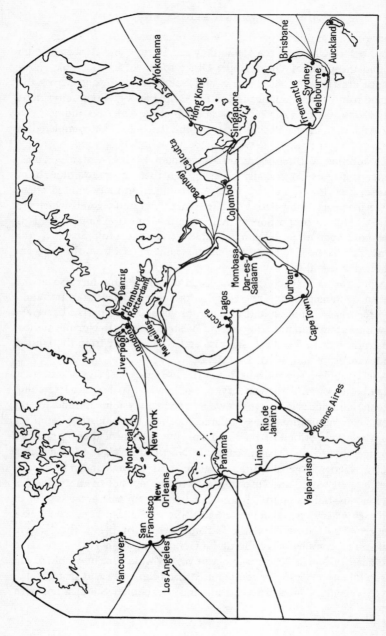

Fig. 55. The World. Major Sea Routes and Ports

In Western Europe inland transport is of great importance in certain areas. The greatest routeway is the Rhine, which is able to take large barges from the North Sea coasts to Switzerland. It enables heavy imports to be brought in more cheaply than would otherwise be possible, and, together with its major tributaries, links together many large industrial regions. The most important of these are Lorraine and the Ruhr, and the canalisation of the Moselle completed in 1964 has made possible the transport of coal and iron ore all the way between them by water (Chapter 6). Other long internal waterways in Western Europe are the Seine, the Meuse, the Rhône and the Dortmund-Ems and Kiel Canals.

LAND TRANSPORT

The greater part of the transport of goods by land takes place either within individual countries or between adjacent countries. Its two most important forms are *roads and railways*. These two are to a large extent complementary, although in many circumstances they are now competitive with one another.

It is usual for heavy and long-distance goods to be taken by rail, since railways have the best facilities for bulk handling. They are of particular importance in a large country such as the Soviet Union, where rail transport dominates the internal movement of raw materials. In areas having low standards of living, and with relatively simple economies, railways are also an excellent general-purpose means of communication. They provide a basic communications network and primary produce for export can be taken by rail speedily and efficiently to the ports.

Road transport on a large scale has only developed in the last forty years, and its chief importance is still for the movement of lighter goods over relatively short distances. It has the advantage of being very flexible and so able to serve a larger number of purposes than is possible for rail. It is well adapted to taking consumer goods from the manufacturers to widely spread markets.

The relative importance of road and rail transport varies greatly depending on the local economic conditions. Railways remain the basic means of transporting goods long distances in large countries with simple economies, but in complex and highly developed countries they have to be supplemented by a road network which is able to penetrate more deeply into all parts. In these and other countries road transport has also been widening its scope by taking heavier goods and covering longer distances. Motorways, in particular, are well able to compete with the railways for long-distance freight. Notable among long-distance motorways are the trans-Canada highway completed in 1964 which now brings road transport to areas previously served by rail. The great Pan-American highway stretching from Alaska to Chile is providing a trunk routeway through the Americas for the first time. In Europe, Germany was the first country to undertake the building of motorways, but now many have been built in all the Western European countries.

For more specialised purposes, *pipelines* are of importance. In North America they are widely used to transport oil, gas and even liquefied coal. They compete very favourably in cost with other forms of transport, and in the United States the mileage of natural gas pipelines alone now exceeds that of railways (see p. 78).

TABLE 12. *Average cost of transporting a barrel of oil over 160 km (100 miles) in the USA*

TANKER	1·5 to 1·8 cents
BARGE	1·75 ,,
PIPELINE	1·9 ,,
RAIL	11·0 to 16 ,,
ROAD	80 ,,

In Europe there are far fewer pipelines than in the United States, but they are used considerably for moving petroleum inland from the importing ports. In the Soviet Union and the Middle East also, much petroleum and gas is moved in this way. In the latter area the main long-distance pipelines are from the producing fields in Iraq and around the Persian Gulf to the Mediterranean (Fig. 22). While the longest of these is about 1,600 kilometres (1,000 miles), the distance from the exporting points on the Persian Gulf to the Mediterranean by sea is 4,800 kilometres (3,000 miles). In spite of this advantage pipelines have not developed greatly in the area, partly due to political difficulties and partly because large tankers are such efficient bulk carriers.

Another important method of transporting power is *electricity transmission lines*. These link the producing and the consuming regions, making electricity available where and when it is needed. Although most transmission from the power station to the consumers is over a short distance, in some cases the distances are considerable. There is a large international exchange of power, such as that of hydro-electric power from Canada to the United States and from Switzerland to its neighbours.

AIR TRANSPORT

This is mainly concerned with the moving of passengers, and it is only competitive for freight if the latter is light and expensive enough to be able to stand the high tariffs. Such things as bullion, precious stones, currency and printed matter are frequently transported in this way, and in the USSR and Western Europe fruit and early vegetables are sometimes sent by air also.

The world's air services are dominated by giant companies such as Pan-American, BOAC, Air France and Aeroflot, although most countries now have their own national airlines. There are two types of air service:

1. Long-distance flights between continents. The most important routes for these bear marked resemblances to the sea routes, but the aircraft are able to shorten distances considerably. This can be readily seen by a comparison of the air and sea routes between Europe and the Far East (Fig. 56). Outstandingly the most important international air route is that across the North Atlantic; others are those from Europe to Africa and from North to South America. On the globe, the shortest distance between two points is the 'Great Circle' line, and aircraft are able to take full advantage of this in shortening distances travelled. The transpolar air routes have now cut distances considerably among the countries of the northern hemisphere industrial belt.

2. Short distance and internal air flights. Internal air transport is most highly developed in the USA and the USSR. Due to the nature of these two vast countries it is a particularly suitable form of communication. In Western Europe also there is an established network of air routes which connect the main centres. Internal air transport is of very great importance to those countries whose very size and under-development make other forms of transport extremely difficult. In

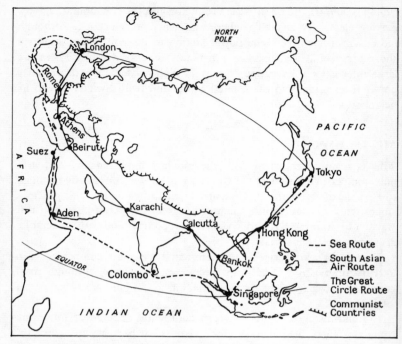

Fig. 56. Sea and Air Communications between London and Tokyo

parts of South America, Africa and Asia, air communications have
come into use before land routes have been established at all.

THE TRANSPORT SYSTEM OF GREAT BRITAIN

In this small and highly industrialised country all the main means of
transporting commodities are used. Waterways and internal airways,
however, take only a very small proportion of the traffic. The most
important internal waterway is the Manchester Ship Canal, and others
still used considerably are the Lea Navigation and the Trent and Mersey
Canal. The road and rail networks dominate the transport system and
are in competition in many fields. The country's main railway lines
radiate from London to the West, Wales and the North, and those
running north divide on either side of the Pennines and extend to

Scotland. The greatest amounts of freight are carried by the railways in the heavy industrial areas of the North. In the south of the country larger quantities are transported by road. Here the road network is denser, and light manufactured goods can readily be transported in this way. The main competitors of the railways for long-distance traffic are the trunk roads and the motorways. The main lines of the motorways now link the south with the industrial regions of the north and north-west.

The transmission of electricity is very flexible as a result of the National Grid which aims to ensure an even distribution from the producers to the consumers. As the greater part of British electricity generation is by coal-fired power stations, there is a considerable surplus in the north of the country. As a result of this most movement is towards the deficient areas of the south and south-east.

The amount of material transported by pipelines is still quite small, but they are now in considerable use to move petroleum from the terminals to the refineries. There are now pipelines from Milford Haven to Llandarcy and Finnart to Grangemouth, and longer ones are connecting Fawley with Avonmouth, and London and the Isle of Grain with the Midlands.

PORTS

A port is the terminal point of a routeway, and it is also the connecting link between one form of transport and another. After goods have arrived at a seaport they may be transhipped on to barges or taken to the railhead to continue their journey. Similarly on arrival at an airport, passengers and freight may be taken to their destination by road. If such terminals are to carry out their function of assisting the efficient movement of goods, they must have the necessary advantages for doing so, and these vary greatly with the type of transport with which they are concerned.

Seaports

The coastlines of the world are dotted with ports, large and small, ranging from tiny fishing harbours to giant liner terminals. The greater part of the world's trade, however, is concentrated in about fifty or so large ports which have grown to their present importance because they possess attributes which have enabled them to outdistance competitors in the amount and value of their trade.

A competitive commercial port needs to have both a good site and a good position. The site should be protected, with ample space for docking facilities, warehouses and ancillary communications. Its approaches must be safe for vessels, and deep enough to enable them to come right in to the coast. This is usually done with the help of the tides, so a high tidal range can be a great boon in areas which would otherwise be too shallow. As to its position, the larger the hinterland, that is the area which it serves, the greater and more varied will be its possibilities for trade. There should be as little natural obstruction as possible to good communications with the hinterland. A port possessing all these advantages would be fortunate indeed, but the world's greatest ports do have them to a large degree.

In terms of total trade the six largest seaports on the North American continent are:

TABLE 13. *Total trade* (*imports and exports*)
(million tons)

NEW YORK	144·8
NEW ORLEANS	61·3
HOUSTON	56·5
PHILADELPHIA	41·0
NORFOLK	38·2
BALTIMORE	37·8

It will be seen that by far the largest of these is New York (Fig. 57). Its annual trade makes it the largest port in the world. Its main imports consist of raw materials and tropical produce, and its exports are of manufactured articles and temperate foodstuffs. There are many other large ports on the Atlantic seaboard of the United States, the main ones being Philadelphia, Norfolk, Baltimore and Boston, but the trade of New York is as much as all these combined. Its nearest rival, Philadelphia, has little more than a quarter of its turnover of merchandise. This dominance is mainly the result of almost unrivalled natural advantages. The natural harbour is large and well protected, and the islands and

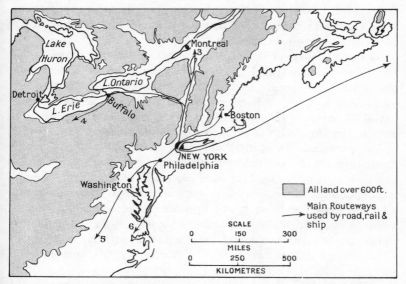

Fig. 57. The Position of New York. *Major routes:* 1. Great Circle route to Western Europe. 2. To New England. 3. Hudson–Champlain Gap to the St Lawrence. 4. Hudson–Mohawk Gap to the Mid West. 5. Main route via the Appalachian Piedmont to the Middle Atlantic and the South. 6. Route along East Coast via the Chesapeake Bridge and Tunnel (opened in 1964)

rivers around it provide a long coastline for wharfs. Its water is deep enough to take the largest ocean liners, and the small tidal range enables ships to enter and leave continuously.

One of the prime causes of its spectacular growth has been its position as a western terminal on the Great Circle Route from Europe, but many adjacent cities also share this advantage. The port's hinterland is the whole of the north-east of the United States for which it is the largest importer and exporter. In serving this huge area it has outstripped its rivals because it is at the seaward end of two of the best routeways through the Appalachian mountains – the Hudson–Mohawk and the Hudson–Champlain gaps. The first of these is the main link between the Atlantic seaboard and the Mid-West, while the second leads to the St Lawrence lowlands of Canada.

The opening of the St Lawrence Seaway has considerably lessened the natural advantages of New York as the natural entry point of goods destined for the interior of North America, but this great city, with its population of 14 millions, has now too powerful a momentum of its own to have been greatly affected.

On the other side of the Atlantic no port has the predominance of New York. This is both because of the greater volume of Europe's foreign trade, and because each nation has developed ports to serve its own needs. The largest European port is Rotterdam which between 1950 and 1965 more than quadrupled its total trade, bringing it up to a tonnage of 130 million tons. It is situated in the southern Netherlands, on one of the mouths of the Rhine and eighteen miles from the sea. As we have already seen this river is a natural avenue of entry into the Continent, but it has long been handicapped by the fact that its course takes it through four countries. Rotterdam has taken advantage of the economic unity which has grown up since the Second World War to build up its trade, and its hinterland now takes in the whole of the Rhineland. It is also in a central location to deal with the trade of the Benelux countries. In response to these developments the appropriately

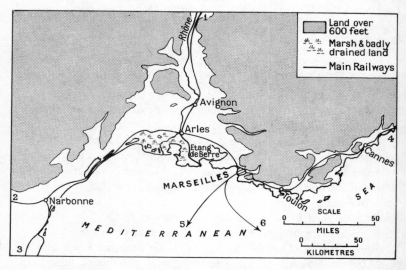

Fig. 58. The Site and Position of Marseilles. 1. Rhône–Saône Corridor to Paris and Northern Europe. 2. The Carcassonne Gap to South-West France. 3. To Spain. 4. To Italy. 5. Sea route to North Africa. 6. To the Eastern Mediterranean and Suez Canal

named 'Europoort' has been constructed on its seaward side in order to take the increases in trade.

The other most important ports on the Continent are Antwerp, Hamburg, Marseilles, Genoa and Le Havre. Antwerp benefits from a central location in relation to the industrial areas of Benelux and Western Germany, and in many ways is a rival to Rotterdam. On the Mediterranean, the 'back door' of Western Europe, the two principal rivals are Marseilles and Genoa. Both of them have expanded their trade rapidly, especially as importers of raw materials. Due to the constriction in the harbour of Marseilles, considerable new growth has taken place at the Etang de Berre to the west of it (Fig. 58). Until the early 1960s Hamburg was the Continent's third largest port, but its trade is now under two-thirds of that of Marseilles. Its growth has been much slower than that of the other main ones, because of the partition of Germany it has lost a great part of its hinterland. Le Havre receives large quantities of goods which are transhipped to barges to be sent up the Seine to Paris. Europe's most important river port is Duisburg-Rohrort at the junction of the Rhine with the Ruhr industrial region.

Entrepôts

These are ports which import goods with the intention of re-exporting them. They are, in effect, assembly points along the shipping routes, situated so as to be able to receive goods conveniently from the producers. Among the most important of these are Singapore, Hong Kong and Colombo, which tranship Far Eastern produce destined for Europe and North America (Fig. 59). Many other ports, like London and Rotterdam, also have a certain entrepôt function.

The Ports of Great Britain

The most important British ports in terms of total tonnage are London, Southampton and Bristol in the south, and Liverpool (with Merseyside), Newcastle and Glasgow in the north. In addition to these there are a large number of smaller ones and specialist ports concerned with only one product, like oil.

Britain's largest port, and the second in Europe, is London, which has an annual trade of 60 million tons. Its principal imports are petroleum, tea, butter, meat, softwood and wool, and it exports among

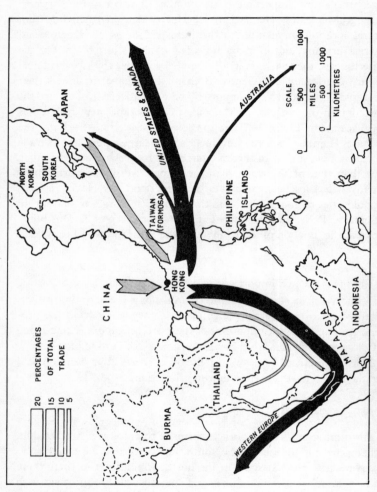

Fig. 59. The Entrepôt Function of Hong Kong. Sources and destination of selected imports and exports are shown as percentages of total trade (imports from the United Kingdom and United States are not included on the map)

other things motor vehicles, engines, components, printed matter and refined sugar. The imports exceed the exports in tonnage by four to one, and this illustrates the port's role as importer for an industrial region which is deficient in most of its requirements in raw materials and food. Southampton deals with both passengers and freight. It has the advantage of deep water and four tides a day, and this, together with its proximity to London, has made it a major British terminal for trans-Atlantic liners and for giant oil-tankers. Bristol is an old port which suffers from being unable to take large vessels. Its imports are specialist, notably wines, sugar and tobacco. Liverpool and Merseyside specialise in the import of raw cotton, oils and fats, chemicals and petroleum for the local industries, and in the export of the finished textile, engineering and chemical products. The South Wales ports bring in heavy goods such as iron ore, petroleum and non-ferrous metals for the region's industries. Formerly Cardiff was the world's largest exporter of coal, but now trade has shrunk to very small proportions. Newcastle and the North-East ports still export coal and other heavy goods, and Glasgow imports many of its region's industrial requirements.

The following are the main specialist types of ports:

PACKET STATIONS. These are ports situated at the terminals of short sea routes. The most important are those which link South-East England with the Continent, such as Dover, Folkestone and Newhaven. These link with continental packet stations such as Ostend, Calais, Boulogne, and Dieppe. On the west coasts of Wales are Fishguard and Holyhead which connect with Wexford and Dun Laoghaire (Kingston) in Ireland.

OUTPORTS. These are points at which cargoes or passengers are unloaded in order to avoid having to take them all the way into the port. This may be done to gain speed or because the port is unable to take vessels above a certain size. An example of an outport of this kind is Avonmouth, eight miles downstream from Bristol. The unloading of heavy goods on the Thames estuary below London is also outport development.

OIL TERMINALS are a highly specialised type of port and have been dealt with on p. 76.

FISHING PORTS. The most important of these in Britain are Grimsby, Yarmouth, Hull and Fleetwood. They are sited in good positions in relation to fishing grounds, and also have good communications with the main centres of population.

Airports

Aircraft are not confined as are ships to the coasts, and the largest airports are clustered in the vicinity of great centres of population. Modern airports taking large airliners need an immense amount of space, with the land flat and suitable for taking the great weights of the aircraft. There must also be good communications with the cities they are serving, and this means that they have to be as near to them as possible. Yet they are unable to get very close because this might mean a lack of space for expansion and make the noise levels unacceptable. Local climate also has to be taken into account, since such things as proneness to fog and frost would restrict use.

In terms of total passengers the largest airports in Western Europe are those of London, Paris, Copenhagen, Frankfurt and Rome. These are natural places for aircraft to land, both on account of the large populations in the surrounding areas, and because of their central locations. London has the world's largest international traffic, which uses Gatwick and Heath Row airports. It is situated on the main line of air travel between North America and Europe, and its importance is now reinforced by the Great Circle and Polar air routes.

WORLD TRADE

In the light of this survey of transport the main features of present-day world trade can now be summarised. Trade in the individual commodities was dealt with under their various headings, so it will be enough now to concentrate on the essential pattern.

1. The greatest importers and exporters are the industrial countries of the Northern Hemisphere, which account for 90 per cent in value of all goods entering into world trade. The countries of the North Atlantic alone take two-thirds of the world's imports (Fig. 60).

2. A large proportion of this trade consists of the imports of primary produce by the manufacturing countries, who in exchange export finished goods to the primary producers.

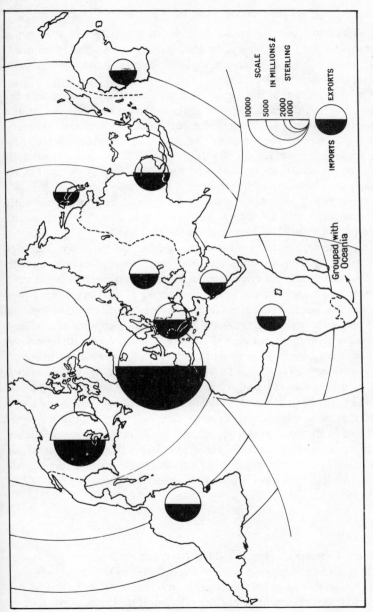

Fig. 60. Value of World Trade by Region 1963. Regional boundaries are shown by dotted lines. The trade total for Asia does not include that of China

3. The manufacturing countries carry on considerable trade among themselves, this being both in finished goods and in primary produce.

4. There is a small volume of trade in foodstuffs and raw materials among the primary producers.

The composition of the exports and imports of any country will depend upon how its trade is spread out over the above categories. In the industrial countries of Western Europe foodstuffs and raw materials make up a large proportion of the imports, while finished goods constitute a large section of the exports. In the case of the United Kingdom in 1963, 35 per cent of its imports were foodstuffs, and 43 per cent of its exports were made up of transport equipment and machinery. By 1968 while the export pattern remained similar, the proportion of foodstuffs in the import total was down to 24 per cent and there had been a considerable increase in imports of manufactured goods.

The same basic pattern is found in the other industrialised countries of Western Europe, although the proportions vary in accordance with the national needs and resources. In France, food imports make up a smaller proportion (14 per cent) on account of her large home production, but her fuel deficit makes the imports of this go up to some 14 per cent of the total. On the other hand, France's exports of food and beverages make up 17 per cent of her total, as compared with only 6 per cent for the United Kingdom and 24 per cent for the Netherlands.

Very different are the patterns of external trade in countries with a large primary production. Canada's trade is in many ways the opposite of that of the United Kingdom: 50 per cent of its imports are of machinery and transport equipment, and only 7 per cent are foodstuffs; in its exports, on the other hand, foods and raw materials make up 40 per cent of the total. In India and Ghana foods make up 30 per cent and 65 per cent respectively of exports, while manufactured goods are 55 per cent and 65 per cent of the imports in each case.

Current World Trends

The most significant trends which have occurred in the pattern of world trade in the period since the Second World War are:

a. While the total value of goods entering into world trade has increased, that of certain among them has increased at a far greater rate

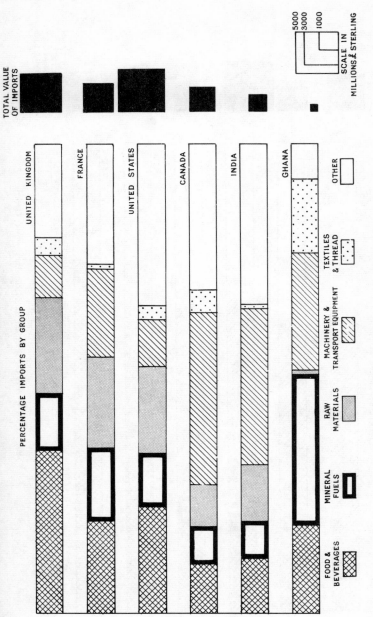

Fig. 61. Exports of Selected Countries by Product Groups

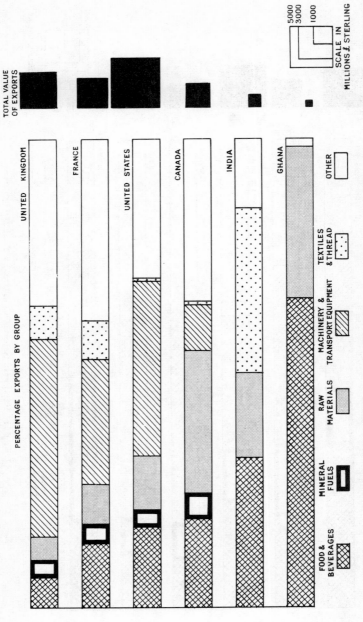

Fig. 62. Imports of Selected Countries by Product Groups

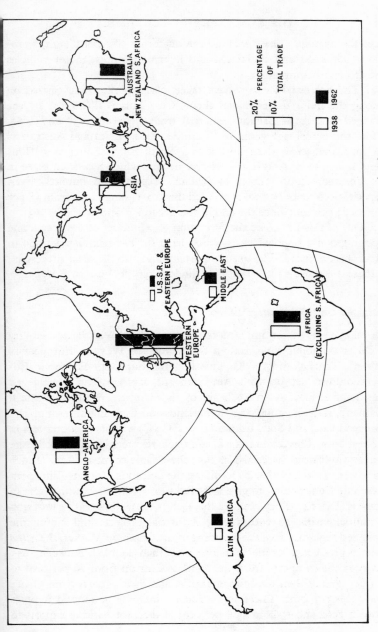

Fig. 63. Destinations of United Kingdom Exports, 1938 and 1962

than the average. These include raw materials like petroleum, ferro-alloys, softwood and chemicals, and in manufactures, motor vehicles and electrical equipment.

b. The greatest increases have taken place in the trade carried on among the industrial countries themselves. This is illustrated by the changed pattern of Britain's external trade between 1938 and 1962. While the percentage going to South America, Africa and Australasia declined, that to Western Europe and North America increased. This trend is also to be seen in the relative decline which has taken place in the Commonwealth's share of Britain's exports and imports. Even imperial preference has not prevented this from going down from 58 per cent to 23 per cent since the end of the Second World War (Fig. 63).

c. Out of this has come the formation of a number of new economic groupings on a regional basis which have further stimulated trade in the areas concerned. The most important, and also the most successful, of these are those which have been undertaken in Western Europe.

Economic Unity in Western Europe

For many years before and after the Second World War the advisability of closer economic links among the nations of Western Europe was realised. To this end the Organisation for European Economic Co-operation was set up with American aid in 1949, and it achieved considerable success. In 1952 six of its members, France, Western Germany, Italy, Belgium, the Netherlands and Luxembourg, set up the European Coal and Steel Community (ECSC) with its headquarters in Luxembourg. This removed tariff and quota restrictions on the exchange of heavy industrial materials. In 1957 these same countries – the 'Inner Six' – went a stage further by founding the Common Market – European Economic Community, to give it its full title – with its headquarters in Brussels (Fig. 64). They pledged themselves to the progressive lowering of mutual tariffs, to encouraging industrial projects and aiding the depressed regions. Since the founding of the Common Market, the gross national product of its members has more than doubled. Between 1955 and 1962 their imports from one another went up from 29 per cent to 37·5 per cent of their total foreign trade, and their exports from 31 per cent to 40 per cent. There was a further increase of mutual imports between 1962 and 1968 to 45·8 per cent of their total and of exports to

Fig. 64. Economic Organisations in Europe

45 per cent. Their economic relations with the rest of Western Europe,
including Great Britain, have also increased, and around 20 per cent of

British overseas trade is now with the Common Market, only slightly less than that with the whole of the Commonwealth.

After the founding of the Common Market, the remaining members of OEEC, consisting of the United Kingdom, Norway, Sweden, Denmark, Austria, Switzerland and Portugal – the 'Outer Seven' – went ahead and founded the European Free Trade Association (EFTA). This is far less ambitious a project than EEC, but trade among its members has been increasing.

The East European countries of Poland, Czechoslovakia, Hungary, Romania, Bulgaria and East Germany are grouped with the USSR into the Council for Mutual Economic Assistance (Comecon) and mutual trade and other ties among them have also been increasing.

CONCLUSION

In this book an attempt has been made to give an outline of the world's present-day economic geography. It has been the writer's aim to show the ways in which man's environment can exert a strong influence on his activities. There are many other factors, economic, social and political, which have also to be considered, but environment is basic.

In the last analysis it is individuals who make the economic decisions. Where to locate a particular factory, in which area to expand production, whether to start up a new plantation – in all these things and many others, a wide choice usually presents itself. The test of whether the right decision has been made in such cases is whether the enterprise turns out to be a success or not. This will depend not only on the enthusiasm of those responsible for building, farming, selling or whatever it may be; it will depend perhaps more on the suitability of the region chosen, from the points of view of its climate, relief, soils, accessibility and mineral wealth; and not only physical factors, but the human environment as well. Labour supply, available markets, transport and political system are all very real influences.

In today's world it is very necessary that all this should be well understood and borne in mind at all levels of economic activity. Policies and decisions made in ignorance of environmental conditions might succeed, but they are far more likely to fail. It is hoped that this book has at least given the student an idea of this geographical background which will be of real use, and may encourage him to study further the interaction between mankind and the varied and fascinating world which is his home.

STUDENT WORK

1. Compare and contrast the main features of the internal transport systems of West Germany and Great Britain, relating your observations to the geographical background in each case.
2. Attempt to explain why rail transport is of greater importance in the USSR than it is in the USA.
3. Contrast the main features of the railway systems of West Africa and India, explaining the differences you find.
4. On an outline map of the world, plot the total tonnages of the world's major merchant fleets in 1962 and 1968, using an appropriate method. Comment on the information revealed by your map, and compare and contrast it with the shipbuilding output of these countries.

	Total tonnage (million metric tons)	
Country	1962	1968
UNITED KINGDOM	21·6	21·9
UNITED STATES	23·1	19·6
FRANCE	5·2	5·7
WEST GERMANY	5·0	6·5
JAPAN	10·0	19·6
LIBERIA	11·4	14·7
NETHERLANDS	5·2	5·3
NORWAY	13·7	19·7
PANAMA	3·9	5·1
SWEDEN	4·1	4·8

5. What differences do you note between the main sea and air routes around southern Asia? State the effects these differences have on the communications system of the area (Fig. 56).
6. Draw sketch maps to illustrate the port functions of New Orleans, Philadelphia and Montreal. Comment on the information which your maps reveal.
7. Using sketch maps to illustrate your answer, compare and contrast the positions and sites of Marseilles and Genoa as importers of raw materials for Western Europe.

8. In what way does the geographical background to the Common Market countries favour their closer economic unification?

9. Why is trade among the industrial nations of the world increasing more rapidly than is the world's trade as a whole?

10. Describe the main methods which can be used to transport petroleum, and give examples to show the best ways in which each can be used.

11. Compare and contrast the main features of the external trade of the United Kingdom and Japan, and explain the causes of the main differences you find.

World Climates

IT is intended that the student should consult this appendix in order to get fuller information on the climatic backgrounds to the production of agricultural raw materials and foodstuffs. The first part of it consists of a brief description of each of the world's major climatic types. This is followed by a table giving the average temperature and rainfall figures for a number of sample stations selected to illustrate each of the climates dealt with. The climatic regions and the sample stations may be easily located by reference to Figs. 65 and 66.

In the description temperatures are given in degrees centigrade with the fahrenheit equivalents in brackets thus: 13° (55°). In the table of sample stations the temperatures are given in fahrenheit only, and rainfall is in inches.

DESCRIPTION OF CLIMATES

Equatorial (low-lying areas within 10° North and South of the Equator)

The basic features of this climate result from the near-overhead position of the sun throughout the year. These features include low atmospheric pressure, high temperatures and humidity, and heavy rainfall. Temperatures average between 24° and 29° (75° and 85°); annual rainfall exceeds 1,500 mm (60 inches) and is frequently much higher. One of the main distinguishing features of this climate is the almost total lack of any real seasons, and conditions remain substantially the same throughout the year. The largest temperature ranges are those between day and night, and these can be as much as 12° (20°). This climate gives rise to the fullest development of tropical rain forest.

Tropical (between 10° and 15° North and South of the Equator and in some equatorial highland regions)

This climate is found between that of the Equator and the Hot Deserts. As a result of the movement of the world's wind and pressure belts together with the movement of the overhead sun, the tropical regions have a transitional climate which is markedly seasonal in character. Temperatures are still very high, and the annual range varies from as little as 6° (10°) on the equatorial side to 18° (30°) on the desert side. In the same way the total rainfall decreases steadily from the equatorial to the desert margins. In the continental interiors there are two distinct seasons. In the warm season when the sun is overhead, or nearly so, there is an 'equatorial' regime with heavy rainfall and uniformly high temperatures. On the other hand, in the cool season – this being very much of a relative term in these areas – the trade winds bring dry sunny weather with low humidity. On the eastern coasts, however, is found the tropical maritime variety. The trades now come in from the sea bringing rain. Rain therefore falls throughout the year, but it is heaviest in the warm season, and the total annual averages from 1,000–1,500 mm (40 to 60 inches) are heavier than in the continental regions.

The natural vegetation of the Tropical Continental is tall savanna grassland, and of the maritime areas a type of tropical rain forest.

Desert (the centres and west coasts of continents astride the tropics and in parts of the interiors of mid-latitude continents)

The deserts are generally considered as those areas having less than 250 mm (10 inches) annual rainfall. They are caused by the high pressures in these regions together with the prevailing landward winds (the trades) which bring little rain. They can be subdivided into the hot and the cold types. The hot deserts are those found on or very near to the tropics. Hot season averages of up to 38° (100°) are experienced in some parts, and annual ranges are large. These regions are also characterised by great temperature extremes, especially between day and night. The very small rainfall is notoriously unreliable and there is frequently considerable fluctuation between one year and another. In some maritime deserts such as the Namib (South Africa) and the Atacama (South America) there is considerable fog, and as a result temperatures may be kept surprisingly low and ranges small. In these maritime deserts the

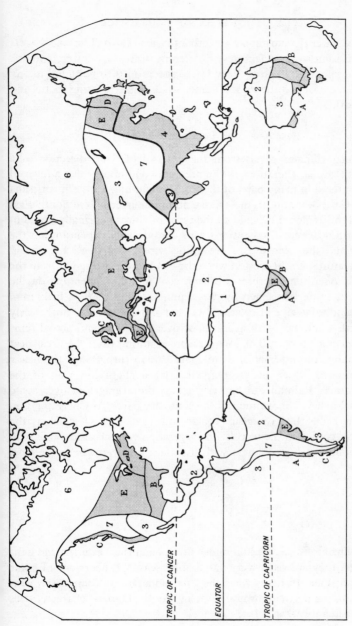

Fig. 65. The Climatic Regions of the World. The areas shaded are those experiencing temperate and monsoon climates (monsoon regions with a thick line drawn around them). In these areas live three-quarters of the world's population. *Climates*: 1. Equatorial. 2. Tropical. 3. Desert. 4. Monsoon. 5. Temperate. A. Warm Western Maritime. B. Warm Eastern Maritime. C. Cool Western Maritime. D. Cool Eastern Maritime. E. Continental. 6. Cold. 7. Mountain

rainfall is lower than in almost any other place on earth. The cold deserts have the same sort of features, but temperatures are lower, and the ranges are generally better. Very little vegetation is to be found in any of these regions, and the typical plants are drought-resisting cactus and thorn bushes.

Monsoon (South-East Asia from Pakistan to Japan)

Monsoonal climates result from the reversal of wind direction as a result of seasonal alterations in the pressure conditions. Such a reversal is encountered in many parts of the world, including northern Australia and the Caribbean, but its most outstanding occurrence is in South-East Asia. In this region it eclipses all the types of climate normally found in these latitudes. Actual conditions vary considerably depending on the latitude and the exposure to prevailing winds, but there are certain typical features. In the winter, when the winds are blowing out from the centre of Asia, temperatures are from cool to cold, depending on the amount of protection given by the mountains, and there is little rain. These conditions give place steadily to hot and dry weather in the early part of the summer, with averages of over 27° (80°) and actual temperatures much higher. The low pressure resulting from the great heat brings about the reversal of winds, and this in turn brings the heavy summer rains which are accompanied by a slight lowering of the temperatures. Rainfall can be very heavy, the averages of over 2,540 mm (100 inches) are common in the southerly parts. At Cherrapunji in northern India the average is 10,820 mm (426 inches) which is the heaviest recorded in the world. The vegetation varies considerably with the rainfall, but mixed forest with luxuriant undergrowth is the most common.

Temperate

These climates are centred on mid-latitudes and the westerly wind belt. However, they are made very variable by seasonal incursions of polar and tropical air. In many ways they are moderate by comparison with climates to the north and south of them, but the climatic characteristics vary considerably from place to place.

WARM TEMPERATE WESTERN MARITIME (Mediterranean, California, central Chile, South Africa, south-west and south-east Australia). This is more commonly known as the 'Mediterranean' climate. It is located in between the tropical high pressure and the mid-latitude low pressure belts, and it is affected by both of these during the course of the year. In the summer the high pressure brings hot and dry conditions with high sunshine rates and temperatures averaging between 21° and 27° (70° and 80°). Winters, by contrast, are cool and moist with average temperatures of between 4° and 10° (40° and 50°) although very cold dry spells can be caused by winds from the interior. Annual rainfall is generally between 500 and 900 mm (20 and 35 inches) and over three-quarters of it normally comes during the winter months. The natural vegetation consists of bushes and trees which are adapted to a low rainfall and long periods of drought.

WARM TEMPERATE EASTERN MARITIME (south of the United States, south-east Africa, south-east Australia). In each part of the world where this is found it is somewhat different. Like the Mediterranean it is transitional, but its location on the opposite sides of the continents gives it very different characteristics. In both seasons average temperatures are higher, with summers between 24° and 30° (75° and 85°) and winters from 7° to 13° (45° to 55°). Rainfall is also heavier, being invariably over 1,000 mm (40 inches) and falling in all seasons. Both seasons have their extremes, with periods of great cold in winter, and of searing heat in the summer. The dominant vegetation is mixed forest with a large number of coniferous trees.

COOL TEMPERATE WESTERN MARITIME (north-west Europe, western coasts of Canada and north-west USA, southern Chile, south Australia, Tasmania, New Zealand). This climate is in the centre of the mid-latitude low pressure region, and experiences on-shore westerly winds for most of the year. These generally bring cool summers and mild winters, and average temperatures are in the range from 2° to 18° (35° to 65°). Rain falls throughout the year, but its amount varies considerably according to altitude and exposure. In Great Britain alone the range is from below 500 mm (20 inches) in parts of the south-east to over 3,810 mm (150 inches) in the mountains of the north-west. In winter the equatorwards extension of polar air can bring very cold and

Sample Stations of the Climatic Types Referred to in Appendix I

First Line: Average monthly temperatures in degrees fahrenheit.
Second Line: Average monthly rainfall in inches.

	J	F	M	A	My	J	Jy	Au	S	O	N	D	ANNUAL RANGE
EQUATORIAL Singapore	79	80	81	81	81	81	81	81	81	80	80	79	3
(Alt. 64 ft.) [19·5 m]	9·9	6·8	7·6	7·4	6·8	6·8	6·7	7·2	7·7	8·2	10·0	10·1	TOTAL 95
TROPICAL CONTINENTAL Kano	71	75	83	88	87	83	79	78	79	81	77	72	ANNUAL RANGE 17
(Alt. 1,533 ft.) [466·3 m]	0·1	0·1	0·1	0·4	2·7	4·6	8·1	12·2	5·6	0·5	0·1	0·0	TOTAL 34·5
TROPICAL MARITIME Rio de Janeiro	77	78	77	75	72	70	69	69	70	71	73	75	ANNUAL RANGE 9
(Alt. 201 ft.) [61 m]	5·0	4·5	5·5	4·2	3·3	2·3	1·8	1·9	2·6	3·4	4·1	5·5	TOTAL 44·2
HOT DESERT Touggourt	50	55	61	69	77	89	92	90	84	72	60	52	ANNUAL RANGE 42
(Alt. 226 ft.) [69 m]	0·2	0·4	0·5	0·2	0·2	0·2	0·1	0·1	0·1	0·3	0·5	0·3	TOTAL 2·9
COLD DESERT Kashgar	22	31	45	59	69	76	80	78	70	57	41	27	ANNUAL RANGE 58
(Alt. 4,296 ft.) [1,308 m]	0·6	0·1	0·5	0·2	0·3	0·2	0·4	0·3	0·1	0·1	0·2	0·3	TOTAL 3·2

	J	F	M	A	My	J	Jy	Au	S	O	N	D	ANNUAL RANGE
MONSOON Calcutta (Alt. 21 ft.) [6 m]	67	71	81	86	86	85	83	83	84	81	74	67	19
	0·4	1·2	1·4	1·7	5·5	11·7	12·8	12·9	9·9	4·5	0·8	0·2	TOTAL 63
WARM TEMPERATE WESTERN MARITIME (Mediterranean) Rome (Alt. 168 ft.) [51·5 m]	44	46	51	56	64	71	76	76	70	62	53	46	32
	3·5	3·1	3·0	3·2	2·3	1·9	0·9	0·9	2·9	5·4	4·7	4·7	TOTAL 34·8
WARM TEMPERATE EASTERN MARITIME Montgomery (Alabama) (Alt. 201 ft.) [61 m]	49	51	58	65	73	80	82	81	77	66	56	49	33
	5·1	5·5	6·3	4·7	3·9	4·1	4·7	4·0	3·1	2·4	3·5	4·7	TOTAL 52·0
COOL TEMPERATE WESTERN MARITIME London (Alt. 18 ft.) [5·4 m]	40	40	44	48	54	60	64	63	58	51	44	41	24
	2·1	1·5	1·5	1·8	1·8	1·7	2·4	2·2	2·0	2·2	2·5	2·1	TOTAL 23·9
COOL TEMPERATE EASTERN MARITIME New York (Alt. 314 ft.) [96 m]	31	31	38	49	60	69	74	73	69	59	44	35	43
	3·7	3·8	3·6	3·2	3·2	3·3	4·2	4·3	3·4	3·5	3·0	3·6	TOTAL 43

	J	F	M	A	My	J	Jy	Au	S	O	N	D	ANNUAL RANGE	TOTAL
WARM TEMPERATE CONTINENTAL Chicago (Alt. 824 ft.) [251 m]	24	27	36	47	57	67	73	72	65	54	40	29	49	
	2·0	2·0	2·6	2·8	3·4	3·5	3·3	3·2	3·1	2·6	2·4	2·0		32·9
COOL TEMPERATE CONTINENTAL Orenburg (Alt. 374 ft.) [114 m]	5	7	18	39	59	67	72	67	55	39	24	12	67	
	1·3	0·9	0·7	0·9	1·5	1·8	1·2	1·3	1·6	1·1	1·7	1·5		15·2
COLD Dawson City (Yukon) (Alt. 1,062 ft.) [323 m]	16	11	6	28	47	57	60	55	43	27	2	13	76	
	0·9	0·6	0·6	0·4	1·1	1·2	1·7	1·8	1·3	1·1	1·0	1·0		12·7

dry conditions with snow, while in the summer the polewards extension of the tropical high pressure can bring very warm and sunny weather.

In extreme coastal parts winters are very mild with little frost, and the annual temperature range can be as little as 9° (15°). These conditions are due to the warm air and sea currents, and protection by mountains from cold continental influences.

The natural vegetation is deciduous forest, but there are admixtures of coniferous trees, and heath and moor are typical of higher land.

COOL TEMPERATE EASTERN MARITIME (north-east USA and south-east Canada, northern Japan and Primorsk region of the USSR). This has many similarities to the western maritime, but it is more extreme in its temperatures. In North America the summers are hotter with averages of 18° to 24° (65° to 75°) and the winters colder going down to averages of −4° to 2° (25° to 35°). Here rainfall varies greatly from place to place, but the most typical range is between 890 and 1,150 mm (35 and 45 inches) falling in all seasons, but with a slight summer dominance. Atmospheric humidity is very high in summer, but lower in winter when some precipitation falls as snow. In the Asiatic region the winters are colder and there is far more snow. The monsoonal influences which are still present this far north result in a marked summer rainfall dominance. The vegetation in all these areas is of mixed deciduous and coniferous forest.

TEMPERATE CONTINENTAL (central USA and south-central Canada, Central and Eastern Europe extending into parts of Western Asia, eastern Argentina, Uruguay and south Brazil, central South Africa, parts of southern Australia). This climate is found in temperate latitudes in areas which are not subject to direct maritime influences. Temperature ranges are much greater than they are in comparable latitudes near to the coasts, and annual ranges of 10° to 21° (50° to 70°) are normal. Actual temperatures vary considerably with latitude, and generally they are between −7° and 21° (20° and 70°) annually in the south and −18° and 18° (0° and 65°) in the north. Rainfall varies between 380 and 1,000 mm (15 and 40 inches), with the heaviest in the southern parts. There is a summer dominance, and most of the winter precipitation is in the form of snow. In the drier parts the rainfall is very unreliable and freak weather conditions are common.

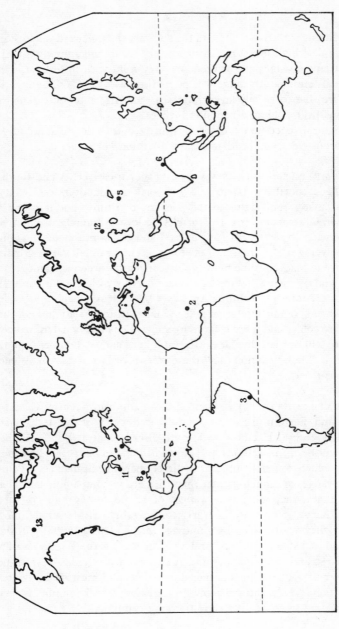

Fig. 66. The Location of Sample Climatic Stations. 1. Singapore. 2. Kano (Nigeria). 3. Rio de Janeiro (Brazil). 4. Touggourt (Algeria). 5. Kashgar (China). 6. Calcutta (India). 7. Rome (Italy). 8. Montgomery (USA). 9. London (Great Britain). 10. New York (USA). 11. Chicago (USA). 12. Orenburg (USSR). 13. Dawson City (Canada)

Short temperate grassland is the characteristic vegetation, but towards the more humid edges there are increasing numbers of trees.

Cold

(Central and northern Canada and Alaska, most of Eurasia north of 60° North.) These areas are situated almost entirely in the region influenced by the Arctic high pressure and the out-blowing Polar winds. Winters are violently cold with averages of below $-18°$ (0°) and in places below $-41°$ ($-40°$). Summers are short, but there might be quite high temperatures over limited periods of time. The precipitation is low, the greater part of it falling as snow. Beyond the Arctic Circle conditions are colder still and only for a few months do average temperatures exceed 0° (32°).

Throughout most of this large area, coniferous forest is the dominant vegetation, but tundra is the only vegetation which will grow around the Arctic fringes.

Mountainous Regions

Temperatures on the average decrease by $1·8°$ (3°) per 305 metres (1,000 feet), and as a result highland and mountainous areas will have climates which are very different from the lowlands in similar latitudes. The lower temperatures will also affect the atmospheric humidity, cloud cover and rainfall totals. In tropical areas the rainfall in such regions will be lower as convection is less liable to occur, while in the temperate regions it will be higher, especially near to coasts, as the rising winds will condense and precipitate.

As a result the high mountainous regions will get very varied climatic conditions depending on their height and latitude. The actual characteristics of any locality will depend on local factors such as the angle and direction of the slopes and the depth of the valleys (see p. 11).

Appendix 2

Metric Conversion Tables

TEMPERATURE		RAINFALL	
1° Fahrenheit = 0·6° Celsius (Centigrade)		1 inch = 25·4 millimetres	
F	C	ins.	mm.
0	− 17·8	1	25·4
10	− 12·2	10	254·0
20	− 6·7	20	508·0
30	− 1·1	30	762·0
40	4·4	40	1016·0
50	10·0	50	1270·0
60	15·6	60	1524·0
70	21·1	70	1778·0
80	26·7	80	2032·0
90	32·2	90	2286·0
100	37·8	100	2540·0

Distance: 1 mile = 1·609 kilometres
Area: 1 acre = 0·404 hectares

Appendix 3

(Note on the Drawing of Maps and Proportional Diagrams)

IT has been said, rightly, that the map is the main tool of the geographer. Well constructed maps supply essential information about the geographical distribution of selected things and their relationship to the distribution of others. Without an understanding of this the world scene can be but imperfectly understood. The student will gain much by drawing his own maps and diagrams at every stage in this course. These 'visual aids' can be of two types:

1. Graphs and proportional diagrams.
2. Sketch maps.

GRAPHS AND PROPORTIONAL DIAGRAMS

The aim of these is to represent information in such a way as to make its meaning much more clear and to bring out new facts about it. For geographical purposes they are used most effectively in conjunction with maps. Some important techniques for our purposes are given below:

LINE GRAPH (see Fig. 7). This is simply the linear plotting of a series of figures so as to bring out their relationships to one another. It is most useful for showing changes occurring over a number of years in such things as commodity output or total trade.

BAR GRAPH (see Fig. 23). This is useful to show comparisons between a particular production or occurrence in a number of countries or regions. The width of the bar must remain constant, while the height is made proportional to the totals being represented. Further information can be added by dividing the bars. If, for instance, the whole bar represents the total imports of a particular country, the relative importance of the various sources of supply can be shown by means of subdivisions. The diagrams may be of still more value if plotted on an outline map of the regions to which they refer.

PROPORTIONAL SQUARES (see Fig. 11). These have a wide use for showing in a comparative way such things as production, exports, incomes and many other aspects of the economy of a nation or region. They are particularly successful when used on outline maps of regions, countries or other units of area, as they are not too bulky, and are able to show very diverse totals on the same diagrams. In order to construct the squares, first work out the square roots of the figures being used. The sides of the squares will then be drawn proportional to these. In deciding the most satisfactory scale, take note of the largest and the smallest of the square roots, and use these as indices for the size of the squares. Take, for example, the following figures for ships launched in a recent year:

	Number launched	Square root
FRANCE	481	22·0
BELGIUM	77	8·8
PORTUGAL	12	3·5
SPAIN	125	11·1

If the scale chosen is too large then the diagrams will be too bulky, while if it is too small then comparison will be difficult, especially among the small producers. If we decide that one unit shall be $1/20$ inch then France's production will be represented by a square with a side of $1\frac{1}{10}$ inch, and the smallest producer, Portugal, by a $\frac{3\frac{1}{2}}{20}$ inch square.

Squares can also be used to show comparisons on the time scale, with one – or more – squares inside one another, each representing the situation at a particular time. If this technique is used then the squares must be distinguished by shading so as to bring out the desired comparisons (see Fig. 47).

If the diagrams are plotted on an outline map of the area to which they refer, then each square should be as near as possible to the country or territory to which it refers, and ideally completely within its boundaries.

PROPORTIONAL CIRCLES (see Fig. 21). The principle of constructing a proportional circle is exactly the same as that of a square. The units of the square root are now made proportional to the radius of the circle, and smaller circles can be placed inside the larger in order to show further comparative data.

DIVIDED CIRCLES OR 'PIE GRAPHS'. These can be used for the same purposes as divided bars, but they are more convenient especially if there are considerable differences between the largest and the smallest totals. The subdivisions of the total must be converted into degrees of a circle, and then marked off on the circle with a protractor. The circles can be made of constant size, in which case the divisions will be in the form of percentages.

Both the proportional and the divided circles can be most usefully used in conjunction with outline maps which serve to bring out many facts resulting from their geographical location (see Fig. 39).

Various forms of shading are essential for the proper production of all these maps and diagrams. They should be used as little as is compatible with clarity, and in this way will be found to be more effective.

SKETCH MAPS

The sketch map is an altogether different technique. The prime aim of the maps and diagrams we have been considering up to now is the accurate representation of facts so as to prepare the ground for their interpretation geographically. The sketch map, on the other hand, is an attempt to put geographical facts into their context, and so help to explain them. This means that a particular fact or distribution is inserted on a map, and other facts which help to explain it are then added. Fig. 57 illustrates this idea. The geographical fact is New York, and the explanatory facts are the distribution of highlands, the routeways, the nature of the coast and the location of other towns. The success of a sketch map of this sort can be judged less by its accuracy, although this must not be neglected, than by the extent to which it is successful in demonstrating the importance of the various factors involved. Therefore simplicity, clarity and pointedness are the most important of its qualities.

Index and Reference Section

Note. This is a specific and comprehensive index, and the student is recommended to use it freely in his work. It should be of particular value for doing the Student Work sections, when the student can consult it to find information on the subjects with which he is concerned. When treating regional subjects which require a full knowledge of a limited area the index will be found an effective way of referring to aspects which are treated in different parts of the book.